STIGMATA

A Tragedy in Three Acts

by

Carolyn Gage

Stigmata

A Tragedy in Two Acts

Stigmata dramatizes the rise and fall of 17th century, Italian nun Benedetta Carlini, who becomes elected abbess on the strength of her miraculous manifestation of the stigmata, and who is eventually tried by the Inquisition for perpetrating a hoax, as well as committing *peccatum mutum*, the so-called "silent sin" of homosexuality.

Benedetta's story begins at a pivotal point in Catholic history, when the Protestant Reformation was gaining momentum and scientific discoveries were increasingly challenging the superstitions and blind faith of an earlier era. The Council of Trent, in an effort to meet these challenges, had passed measures to discourage the obsession with paranormal manifestations of divine favor.

The play opens with a scene where the teenaged Benedetta is directing a re-enactment of the rape of St. Agnes with her girlfriends. Interrupted by her mother, Benedetta defends her dramatic production by explaining that it is her father who has been responsible for her precocious sexuality. Frantic to place Benedetta in a convent, her mother brings her to a religious order in Pescia, outside Florence. Initially rejecting Benedetta because of her class background, the Abbess changes her mind when she witnesses the mother's abuse. Benedetta fakes her first miracle.

Benedetta becomes the secretary for the Abbess and thrives under her loving mentorship. Given scope for her creativity and ambition, Benedetta has no need for miraculous manifestions. On the eve of their move to a new compound, Benedetta confronts the lesbian dynamic between herself and the Abbess, and the Abbess, in a panic, dies.

At this point, the action shifts to the new convent, where Benedetta's sudden stigmata has resulted in her becoming elected the new abbess. Ricordati, an old-school priest, protects and enables her, and under his tutelage, Benedetta officially encloses the convent and institutes the austere rules of St. Augustine. These strip her rivals of their privilege, institute the practice of whipping, and consolidate her power. She begins to deliver speeches, in the persona of St. Catherine of Siena, to the terrorized nuns. Finally, she announces that it is God's will for her to marry Jesus in a formal, public ceremony.

The night before her "wedding," Benedetta deceives Mea, a convent servant, into submitting sexually to her. She tells the young nun that she, Benedetta, will become possessed by the spirit of a male angel named Splenditello, whom Jesus has sent to marry Mea. Later, at Benedetta's wedding ceremony, the town Provost exposes her as a fraud, and her shocking abuse of another nun is revealed. These revelations prompt Mea to come forward with her story. Benedetta warns the town that God will send the plague if they dare incarcerate her.

The final act of the play transpires at Benedetta's deathbed in her prison cell. The plague has returned to Florence, and the townspeople, who have never lost their awe of "Saint" Benedetta, have gathered in a mob to demand her release, so that she will pardon them and lift the curse. Benedetta, defying her former enemies, collapses when the ghost of her beloved Abbess appears. At her death, her former rival slashes the hands of Benedetta and orders the body, with its new stigmata, be displayed to the superstitious townsfolk.

12 women, 2 men (2 of the women's roles may be double-cast)
Multiple venues
2 ½ hours.

Introduction

In a global environment of rising fundamentalism, it is timely to ask, "What does it take for a woman to keep her sexuality and ambition alive in a repressive, patriarchal culture of female self-abnegation?'

Stigmata, based on the Inquisition records of a 17th century lesbian nun, explores the answers to this question. Benedetta Carlini, a young Italian woman raised with masculine expectations, exploits her theatrical abilities to convince the other nuns and her priest that she is channeling the voices and spirits of a variety of saints, manifesting stigmata and other miracles. Elected abbess on the strength of these miracles, she moves swiftly to impose rules of austerity on the convent, effectively stripping her rivals of their class privilege and consolidating her power.

Finally, in her hubris, Benedetta goes too far, seducing one of the younger nuns by impersonating a male angel named "Splenditello." Her victim, awakened to her sexuality with an ecstatic experience, realizes later that she has been a victim of fraud... or has she?

Benedetta aggressively rejects the culture of confession, abasement, and deprivation that is expected of the women in their patriarchally prescribed roles. Is she perpetrating fraud or creatively manipulating the system to retain her authenticity?

Stigmata challenges audience with a larger-than-life, female heroine from the pages of history—asking us to examine our own collaborations and accommodations in a culture that still expects women to sabotage ourselves and betray our truths.

One of the hallmarks of late-stage recovery from childhood trauma is the ability to tolerate contradiction, to hold simultaneously in consciousness two conflicting ideas. The landscape of trauma appears to be black-and-white, a world of good and evil, predators and prey. As the survivor recovers, she begins to discern the areas of gray—perhaps the victim status of her perpetrators, coexisting with their role as perpetrators. Compassion is the compass for navigating the gray, and with compassion can come a deeper awareness of one's own internal contradictions and an acceptance of them.

Lesbian culture has barely begun to emerge from the trauma of the closet. We have been burned at the stake, banished to convents, locked up in mental asylums for "erotomania," excommunicated, drummed out of the military in disgrace, disinherited, fired, evicted, arrested in our own bars, raped at the police stations. We have been denied our right to legal protections, denied the sanctity of our committed relationships. We have lost custody of our children. Our literary heritage has been fraught with vampiric homewreckers, predatory school mistresses, lonely spinsters, and monstrously insatiable sex addicts. In these narratives, the "happy ending" has usually entailed our death—frequently by our own hand.

Cultures recover from traumatic silence and secrecy in stages that are similar to those experienced by individual survivors. Just as survivors raised in abusive environments pass through a stage of casting off the false identities imposed on them by their perpetrators, so a culture emerging from repression casts off the false stereotypes and paradigms of that oppression. Contemporary lesbian culture has embraced new archetypes of lesbians as heroines, as rescuers of women, as visionary leaders and artists and activists. The world that has historically scapegoated us is thrown into sudden relief, with its brutal history of misogyny and patriarchal control over women's bodies. The narratives have become reversed as the lesbian lover is depicted as the agent of sanity and healthy sexuality. This is cause for celebration, just as it is for the survivor on her way to reclaiming her identity.And, just as with the survivor, there is a further stage of evolution, where this emerging identity becomes robust enough to incorporate contradiction—where lesbian central characters can be both victim and perpetrator, and where we can bear to examine, up-close, the damage—the internalized oppression from surviving a homophobic world—and how this can still manifest in our post-recovery culture.

Stigmata is a play about late-stage cultural recovery. It is about a woman who is both courageous in her resistance and shocking in her perpetration. She finds ingenious ways to keep alive both her ambition and her sexuality in the stultifyingly repressed environment of a 17th-century, Italian convent, where neither are allowed and where self-abasement and self-denial are the order of the day. And, simultaneously resisting and acting out the internalized misogyny of her conditioning, she perpetrates against a sister nun and inmate.

What are we to make of her? The townspeople believe her to be a saint. The Inquisition has branded her a demon. Obviously, she is neither, but can we accept her as both victim and perpetrator?

Benedetta Carlini's story is documented in Judith Brown's book *Immodest Acts*. In her book, Brown cites the court records from the Inquisition, where Carlini's victim testifies about these "immodest acts." Some have been tempted to assume that this woman had been Carlini's partner in a consenting lesbian relationship, but that, called before the Inquisition, she chose to save herself by betraying her lover, insisting that she had been the victim of deception and manipulation.

That might be a plausible theory, except that this witness' testimony is so consistent with contemporary narratives by victims of sexual predators. She describes in vivid detail an escalating campaign of sexual harassment and entrapment by Carlini, a campaign designed to convince her that the perpetrations were, in fact, the will of God.

Carlini, however, was far more than a perpetrator. The trial records include extensive documentation of behaviors that used to be labeled "hysterical behavior," but which trauma therapists today might diagnose as Complex Post-Traumatic Stress Disorder, a syndrome associated with child sexual abuse. Carlini's adeptness at successfully assuming the personae of Jesus, St. Catherine of Siena, and the male angel named "Splenditello" point to a possible history of dissociative identity disorders, another syndrome associated with child sexual abuse. In describing her near-death experience, Carlini claimed to have seen her father in Purgatory, begging her forgiveness. This, along with the fact she perpetrated in a male persona, caught my attention. Was the historical Benedetta Carlini a survivor of paternal incest?

Carlini's spiritual community was not an enclosed order. The Abbess who founded it appeared to be an enlightened woman with feminist ideals. I amplified these themes in the play, and I used the death of the Abbess as the turning point for Carlini's character. Without this powerful mentor and "enlightened witness" to her abuse and to her genius, Carlini resorts to increasingly desperate and manipulative tactics in order to retain her freedom and her status in this microcosm of patriarchally controlled women. With a superstitious priest as her enabler, she takes increasing liberties with her seemingly divinely-ordained authority, provoking increasing jealousy and hostility among the nuns.

At the death of the priest who is Benedetta's protector, these nuns come forward to denounce her, and Carlini finds herself unable to sustain the hoax. Possibly because of her popularity with the townspeople, the Church chose not to execute her, but to imprison her inside the convent for life.

Initial responses to *Stigmata* have ranged from anger that I would choose to "valorize" a perpetrator, to questions about my intended impact on an audience. My response is that I want to present an audience of lesbians and our allies with a lesbian central character who is both survivor and perpetrator, larger-than-life, historical, and complicated. I want to challenge my community to hold all of the contradictions of Benedetta Carlini in consciousness, just as we are learning to hold within ourselves our utopian dreams of sisterhood with our personal histories of betrayal.

I challenge my community to embrace our history, all of our history—with our addictions, which helped us stand the pain even as they caused us to harm each other, with the lies we have had to perpetrate in order to hold onto our select truths, with the crimes we have had to commit in order to survive a world that made it legal to starve us out onto the streets. Most of all, I challenge us, in expanding our capacity for tolerating contradiction, to develop the compassion that is the hallmark of integration from personal and historical trauma.

Cast of Characters

BENEDETTA CARLINI: A lesbian butch survivor of paternal incest; member of a bourgeois family from the mountains.

GINEVRA: A young, teenaged friend of Benedetta's from her village.

TERESA: A young, teenaged friend of Benedetta's from her village.

MIDEA: Benedetta's mother.

PIERA PAGNI: The Abbess of the Congregation of the Mother of God.

PAOLO RICORDATI: A priest, the superstitious confessor of the Congregation of the Mother of God.

STEFANO CECCHI: The worldly Provost for the town of Pescia.

FELICE DI GIOVANNI GUERRINI: A worldly nun at the Congregation of the Mother of God, daughter of one of Pescia's wealthiest families.

MARGHERITA D'IPTOLITO RICORDATI: An alcoholic nun at the Congregation; Father Ricordati's niece.

ANGELINA: A nun at the Congregation of the Mother of God, a survivor of sexual abuse with serious mental illness.

BARTHOLMEA CRIVELLI: A simple convent servant at the Congregation of the Mother of God.

MAURA: An older convent servant at the Congregation, old-fashioned in her faith.

CRISTINA: A cynical nun at the Congregation.

CECILIA BIANCHI: A socially-conforming nun from a wealthy family at the Congregation; Felice's partner.

Synopsis of Scenes

Act I

Scene 1: The interior of Benedetta's bedchamber, January 21 (St. Agnes' Day), 1616, Vellano, Italy.

Scene 2: The interior of the Abbess' office at the Congregation of the Mother of God, winter, 1616, Pescia, Italy.

Scene 3: The interior of the chapel at the Congregation of the Mother of God, same day as previous scene.

Scene 4: The interior of the Abbess' office, same day.

Scene 5: The interior of the chapel, same day.

Scene 6: The courtyard of the Congregation of the Mother of God, March 25 (Annunciation Day), 1618.

Scene 7: The interior of the Abbess' office, same day as previous scene.

Scene 8: The interior of the chapel, same day.

Scene 9: An area to the side of the bridge over the Pescia River, late afternoon of the same day.

Act II

Scene 1: The interior of the new chapel, April 25 (Good Friday), 1618.

Scene 2: The interior of the sacristy of the new chapel, the first week of May, 1618.

Scene 3: The interior of the Abbess' office, May 19 (the eve of Pentacost), 1618.

Scene 4: The interior of the chapel of the Convent of the Mother of God, the Day of the Holy Trinity, 1618.

Scene 5: The interior of the sacristy, a few hours before the scheduled wedding.

Scene 6: The interior of the new chapel, minutes before the wedding.

Act III

Scene 1: The courtyard of the Convent of the Mother of God, Ascension Day, 1631.

Scene 2: The office of the Abbess of the Convent of God, the same day.

Scene 3: The interior of Benedetta's cell, the same day.

ACT I

Scene 1

The interior of BENEDETTA's bed chamber, January 21, 1611. The room is in an Italian, bourgeois home in the small mountain village of Vellano, located forty-five miles from Florence. GINEVRA, 15, enters. She is a friend of BENEDETTA's, a young village girl. She wears a makeshift beard and is dressed like a man.

GINEVRA: Benedetta... Benedetta! Where are you? We're ready to start! Where are you...?

BENEDETTA: I'm here... *(BENEDETTA, 16, enters. She has very short hair and she is wearing a man's shirt and no pants. She jumps into the bed and pulls the sheets around her. GINEVRA stares.)* What are you staring at? Start the play! *(GINEVRA exits and then re-enters. BENEDETTA pulls the sheets up to her chin, covering herself in mock horror.)*

GINEVRA: *(Reciting her lines.)* "Agnes, I will give you diamonds and great riches if you will consent to be my wife."

BENEDETTA: *(By far the better actor.)* "Begone, sting of sin, food of crime, poison of the soul—for I am already given to another lover! ... Already I have been embraced by his pure arms, already his body is with my body... *(GINEVRA stands mesmerized. BENEDETTA comes out of character.)* Fall down! Faint! *(GINEVRA falls down. TERESA, 15, enters. She is another friend, also dressed like a man, wearing a white beard.)*

TERESA: "My son! My son!"

GINEVRA: "I am dying, Father."

TERESA: *(To BENEDETTA.)* "Agnes, why won't you marry him?"

BENEDETTA: "I cannot break faith with my bridegroom."

1

TERESA: "Who is your lover? What is his name?"

BENEDETTA: "I will not say!"

TERESA: "I shall lock thee up with prostitutes!"

BENEDETTA: "I will not sacrifice to thy gods, and yet I shall not be defiled, for I have with me a guardian of my body, an angel of the Lord!" *(There is an awkward silence. BENEDETTA breaks character again, speaking to TERESA.)* You're supposed to rip off my dress. *(TERESA crosses to the bed and begins to unbutton BENEDETTA's shirt.)* No—! Like this! *(BENEDETTA rips the shirt open and then clutches it to her body in mock terror.)* Now, you take me to the house of the prostitutes... *(TERESA takes her arm and parades her around the chamber. They stop at the bed.)* Throw me on the bed. *(TERESA pushes BENEDETTA toward the bed. BENEDETTA throws herself melodramatically on it with a scream. Both the girls freeze in fascination. BENEDETTA turns to GINEVRA, who is still on the floor.)* Now, you try to rape me, and you—*(To TERESA.)* You be the angel who strangles him.

TERESA: But I'm the father...

BENEDETTA: You were—but now you're the angel! Here... Get behind me on the bed, and I'll lie like this... *(TERESA climbs onto the bed and kneels behind BENEDETTA, who has resumed her former position. BENEDETTA turns to GINEVRA.)* Now, you come in and see me, and you are very excited, because you get to rape me, and you say, "Agnes, now I will have you!' and you try to kiss me, only after you get on top, you—*(To TERESA.)*... try to strangle him! *(GINEVRA gets up, exits, and re-enters.)*

GINEVRA: *(Uncertainly.)* "Agnes, now I will have you!" *(Uncertainly, she gets into bed next to BENEDETTA, but not touching her. She waits to be strangled.)*

BENEDETTA: *(To GINEVRA.)* No! You're supposed to try to rape me! *(GINEVRA doesn't move.)* Here, I'll show you—*(BENEDETTA turns over and simulates the motions of a rapist. Resuming her position as Agnes, she speaks to GINEVRA.)* Go on...*(GINEVRA moves gingerly on top of BENEDETTA and begins to imitate BENEDETTA's movements. BENEDETTA begins to struggle.)* Take my wrists! Tell me to be quiet! *(GINEVRA becomes more boistrous. BENEDETTA struggles more.)*

GINEVRA: Be quiet! Be quiet! Be quiet! *(BENEDETTA lets out a blood-curdling scream. Suddenly, TERESA screams, reaches out, and begins to strangle GINEVRA. Just then the door opens and MIDEA enters. The girls freeze. MIDEA CARLINI is in her forties. She never wanted to have a child, and she has left the raising of her daughter to her husband.)*

MIDEA: Benedetta!

GINEVRA: *(To BENEDETTA.)* It's your mother! *(GINEVRA lets go of BENEDETTA's wrists and jerks away from her. TERESA lets go of GINEVRA's neck.)*

MIDEA: What are you girls doing?

BENEDETTA: It's a religious play. It's the life of St. Agnes.

MIDEA: *(To GINEVRA and TERESA.)* You go home right now! *(The two girls rip off their beards and race out of the room. MIDEA turns to her daughter.)* Put your clothes on!

BENEDETTA: *(Defiant.)* Agnes' hair has grown to cover her.

MIDEA: Well, yours certainly isn't covering anything! *(Slowly and insolently, BENEDETTA gets out of the bed. She begins to pull on her pants in front of MIDEA. MIDEA watches her.)* Where did you get such filthy ideas?

BENEDETTA: *(Quoting from the play.)* "I will not say…"

MIDEA: *(Enraged.)* You will not say? *(She slaps BENEDETTA.)*

BENEDETTA: *(Slowly.)* I read it in a book.

MIDEA: Liar! What book?

BENEDETTA: *The Golden Legend. (Retrieving a book.)* See for yourself. *(She holds it out to her mother.)* Oh, you can't read. I forgot. Shall I read it for you? *(She opens the book and starts to read.)* "Already I have been embraced—" *(MIDEA knocks the book out of her hands and slaps her.)*

MIDEA: Where did you get such a filthy book? *(MIDEA slaps her again.)* Do you want me to tell your father?

BENEDETTA: *(Giving her a strange look.)* You do that.

MIDEA: You think I won't? I told him it was a sacrilege, raising you like a boy! Teaching you to read... and now this... blasphemy!

BENEDETTA: *(Cutting her off.)* Tell him! Go ahead. Oh, and... ... *(She picks up the book from the floor.)*... be sure to give him back his book. *(She picks up the book and extends it to MIDEA. MIDEA stares at her.)*

MIDEA: *(Crossing to the door.)* Devil! Child of the devil!

BENEDETTA: *(Reciting.)* "...already his body is with my body—" *(MIDEA exits and slams the door. BENEDETTA turns away.)*

Blackout

End of Scene

ACT I

Scene 2

Interior of the office of Piera Pagni, ABBESS of the Congregation of the Mother of God, located in the town of Pescia, nine miles from Vellano—but worlds away socially and economically. It is a winter day, 1611. A meeting is in progress between the ABBESS, FATHER PAOLO RICORDATI, who is the confessor for the Congregation, and MONSIGNOR STEFANO CECCHI, provost for the town of Pescia. The ABBESS is a handsome woman in her early fifties. The founder of the pre-convent, she is passionate about her work. FATHER RICORDATI, in his seventies, is an "old school" priest, preferring the age of miracles to the age of enlightenment. CECCHI, a vigorous man in his fifties, has been the town provost for two decades, presiding over its ecclesiastical affairs. He is an ambitious man, and his interest in the Church is purely political.

ABBESS: *(Bending over a large drawing on her desk.)* ... And, as you can see, the new buildings come with six and a half acres of the best land in Pescia... We break ground this month, and should be able to relocate in two years. And this section is going to be cleared for a vegetable garden...

CECCHI: *(Baiting the ABBESS.)* All of this is going to be walled in, of course.

ABBESS: *(Annoyed.)* Of course. The nuns are very particular about not having our vegetables stolen.

CECCHI: I was referring to enclosure of the *entire* community. If the Congregation of the Mother of God were to become an official convent of the Catholic Church, it would mean quite an advancement of status.

ABBESS: An advancement of status for *you*. From town provost to bishop?

RICORDATI: *(Nervously.)* Enclosure would certainly bring many blessings from our Lord.

ABBESS: Father Ricordati, I am well aware of what enclosure brings. I am an abbess, and I have no desire to become a jailer.

CECCHI: Careful, Piera . . .

ABBESS: I *am* careful, Monsignor Cecchi... very careful. The lives of eighteen women are my responsibility, and I take that very seriously. That is why, as long as there is breath in this body, the Congregation of the Mother of God will remain just that—a "congregation." I will never allow it to become enclosed.

RICORDATI: *(A gentle reminder.)* "Not my will, but Thine," Mother Pagni.

ABBESS: Is it really the divine will of a loving Father to see his daughters locked up, denied visitors, denied possessions, denied any and all occupations except prayer and fasting?

RICORDATI: You misunderstand. Enclosure is for the *protection* of the nuns. The Rules of St. Augustine are designed to relieve them of the burden of worldly responsibility. The enclosed convent is a paradise for the girl who has renounced the world to become a bride of Christ. The convent is the enclosed garden, where she can entertain her Beloved in secret places and—in the words of St. Bernard—enjoy the divine caresses which never come in public—

ABBESS: *(Cutting him off.)* Father Ricordati, I know what goes on behind enclosed convent walls as well as you do... Girls trying to outdo each other in starvation, girls cutting themselves to imitate the wounds of Christ—whipping each other into frenzies, wearing horsehair undergarments, sleeping on rocks and nails, refusing to bathe, glorying in disease—the more gruesome the better—as a token of divine favor, and stoking each other's fevered imaginations with pornographic delusions of demonic persecution and hallucinatory organ exchanges...

RICORDATI: *(Indignant.)* If you are referring to St. Catherine of Siena and the Sacred Heart of Jesus—

ABBESS: *(To CECCHI.)* I'll tell you what these girls need—love! That's what they need. Let's tell the truth—These girls don't come here because of a religious calling. They come because their families bring them. And why? Because a nun's dowry is cheaper than a bride's.

RICORDATI: I think we are missing the point here... It is the saints and the miracles that bring people to the Church. Without enclosure, where is the mystery? When the people of the town can see these girls any time they like, eat with them, watch them perform their music in the chapel—they lose their respect—

ABBESS: Respect? I could tell you—you, their confessor—! I could tell you stories about what goes on behind the closed doors of these "respectable" houses... Respect! *(A pause.)* You want a saint? How about Angelina?

RICORDATI: I didn't—

ABBESS: *She* talks to Jesus... *She* sees the Virgin Mary... Sometimes two or three times before breakfast! What about her?

CECCHI: Who is Angelina?

RICORDATI: Monsignor, the Abbess—

ABBESS: A girl who was left tied to the convent gates, naked and raving. She is out of her mind.

CECCHI: And you accepted her as a nun?

ABBESS: Yes, I did. If I had not, she would have been chained up in some madhouse where the same horrors that deprived her of her reason would have been perpetrated against her on an hourly basis. But here, she believes she is in Paradise—and why not? There are no men here.

CECCHI: *(After a pause, pointedly.)* And how is your health, Piera?

ABBESS: Fine. Why do you ask?

CECCHI: Because there were rumors that you had suffered a stroke this winter, and I was just thinking that the girls like Angelina might not find themselves so well-protected with a different Abbess. *(Pausing.)* Without enclosure, that is.

ABBESS: Your concern for us is touching, but I have no intentions of dying any time soon.

RICORDATI: *(Rising in agitation.)* One hundred and fifty years ago, this town was ravaged by plague. Ravaged! One third of Pescia perished. I can still remember my grandfather's descriptions of it, as vivid to me as if I had lived through it myself! First there is the appearance of a swelling the size of an orange, under the arm or, more painful, in the groin—an agonizing, hideous, black, pustulant swelling... harbinger of death, for, then, within just a few hours of this vile bubo, the onset of a fever, followed by vomiting, and skin that burns as if it had been in a fire. And during this visitation of all the afflictions of Job, mysterious markings begin to appear on the surface of the body—tabulations from the Book of Life—! And only when this poor sinner has reached the apotheosis of carnal suffering for the sins of this body, only then, is his reason taken from him, so that even his inevitable death cannot be redeemed by the sanctity of confession—but he must die writhing in his own pollution, unforgiven, his final pronouncements on his evil life no more than the incoherent ravings of a madman. Monsignor Cecchi, Mother Pagni... one out of three. Which of us might it have been?

CECCHI: I think—

RICORDATI *(Cutting him off.)* Where, in their absolute terror and confusion, did the people turn? To the doctors who could only cut the already lacerated, purge the already purging— who could only cauterize the poor devils who were already thrashing in the fires of hell? No! I will tell you where they turned... to the Church! They turned to the Church! They turned to the Saints, the Saints who understood torture, who themselves had died on the rack, on the

Catherine wheel, at the stake! The people did not want doctors, Mother Pagni—*They wanted Saints!* The plague that emptied this town, filled the churches!

CECCHI: They would have done better to look to their rats than to their relics.

RICORDATI: Rats?

CECCHI: The disease appears to be spread by rats.

RICORDATI: *(Thundering.)* The plague, Monsignor Cecchi, was the Scourge of God!

CECCHI: You're out of step with the times, Father. The plague belongs to another century, and so do your saints.

RICORDATI: *(Turning sharply to the ABBESS.)* Mother Pagni, there was a procession in Pescia forty years ago. Do you remember?

ABBESS: *(A weary smile. RICORDATI has told this story many times.)* I was a child.

RICORDATI: Well, I was not, and I remember it well, because I was in that procession. And as we were crossing the bridge over the Pescia River, the Virgin herself suddenly appeared to one of my brother priests. And as he knelt down before Her, there was a light that shone around him. *(CECCHI starts to interrupt.)* I saw it! I saw that light! And so did the people of Pescia. And later they built a shrine to the Virgin right there, in the middle of the bridge. And that shrine was so popular—mark you, Monsignor!—*so popular* that it caused a congestion of the traffic on the bridge so great, it was necessary to move the shrine to another location. That was forty years ago, and that shrine still stands, and people still visit it, and everyone in Pescia—even those who were too young to remember—can tell you the exact spot on the bridge where that miracle occurred. Now, *that* is what keeps the Church strong.

CECCI: *(Turning to the ABBESS.)* Have you given some thought to appointing the Guerrini girl your successor?

ABBESS: Felice?

CECCHI: Her father is your wealthiest benefactor, isn't he?

RICORDATI: *(Shocked.)* Sister Felice is the *least* spiritually-minded of all the nuns!

ABBESS: *(To CECCHI.)* I *have* thought of her. She's educated and extremely ambitious.

RICORDATI: *(Shocked.)* "Ambitious?"

CECCHI: *(Turning to RICORDATI.)* Would you rather see your niece Margherita appointed?

RICORDATI: My niece, sir, is a drunkard and a fool, but that is no reason to appoint the Guerrini girl. I think you forget that Our Lord was a carpenter.

CECCHI: Like your father?

RICORDATI: *(Rising stiffly, to the ABBESS)* Mother Pagni.

ABBESS: Father. *(RICORDATI exits.)*

CECCHI: *(Smiling conspiratorially at the ABBESS.)* He doesn't like to be reminded of his roots.

ABBESS: We are all laborers… *(She rises.)* Provost.

CECCHI: *(Rising with a smile.)* You will think about enclosure?

ABBESS: I assure you I will *not.* *(CECCHI exits. The ABBESS, troubled, returns to her desk.)*

Blackout.

End of Scene

ACT I

Scene 3

The interior of the chapel of the Congregation of the Mother of God, the same day. At the front of the chapel are an altar, a baptismal font, a lectern holding the Holy Scriptures, and a larger-than-life statue of the Virgin Mary. BENEDETTA, 16, wearing men's riding clothes, enters the chapel. Irreverently, she takes stock of her surroundings, handling items on the altar. Crossing to the baptismal font, she bends over and washes her face in it, wiping her hands on the altar cloth. Hearing someone enter the chapel, she conceals herself behind the statue of Mary. MARGHERITA enters. MARGHERITA d'IPTOLITO RICORDATI is a young woman, the niece of Father Ricordati. She is an alcoholic and envious of the girls from more privileged backgrounds.

MARGHERITA: Felice! Felice!

FELICE: *(Entering.)* Keep your voice down! *(FELICE di GIOVANNI GUERRINI, 18, is the daughter of one of Pescia's wealthiest and most prominent families. She is comfortable with her privilege, understanding both the uses and abuses of power.)*

MARGHERITA: *(Rushing up to her.)* Did you get it?

FELICE: Of course. *(FELICE opens her sleeve to reveal a bottle of wine. MARGHERITA grabs for it.)* Not yet! Tell me what you've heard.

MARGHERITA: Let me taste it first.

FELICE: Tell me which of the nuns are going to sign my petition to Mother Pagni.

MARGHERITA: They all are.

FELICE: No, they're not. Tell me who isn't.

MARGHERITA: *(Whining.)* Why do you want to be appointed Mistress of the Novices. It's nothing but more work—training all the new girls. If I were the daughter of Giovanni Guerrini, I'd have myself appointed Mistress of the Cellar.

FELICE: Well, maybe someday I'll become Abbess, and then I'll appoint you Mistress of the Cellar.

MARGHERITA: Really? Would you?

FELICE: I'd have to become Abbess first, and that's not going to happen unless I can establish myself in a position of authority, like Mistress of the Novices. Now—tell me who isn't signing.

MARGHERITA: Well, I asked Lucrezia and Verginia if they were going to sign, and at first they didn't want to do it, but then I reminded them that they both still owed you money from their investiture ceremony— *(MARGHERITA reaches for the bottle. FELICE withholds it.)*

FELICE: And what about Cristina? *(MARGHERITA hesitates.)* What about Cristina? Is she signing?

MARGHERITA: No. *(FELICE waits.)* She says *she* wants to be Mistress of the Novices.

FELICE: *(Musing.)* She's lying, of course. She wants something else. *(To MARGHERITA.)* Did she say what it was?

MARGHERITA: No.

FELICE: I know she said something else.

MARGHERITA: If she did, I can't remember. *(FELICE turns to leave.)* I did what you said! *(FELICE keeps walking.)* Oh, wait—I know! Cristina said that she would make a better Mistress of the Novices, because she sleeps in the dormitory. She said she could keep an eye on the new girls.

FELICE: *(Stopping thoughtfully.)* She wants my room. *(Turning to MARGHERITA suddenly.)* Tell her she can have it. I'll take her bed in the dormitory.

MARGHERITA: You're going to give up the best room in the convent...

FELICE: *(Smiling.)* You can have your bottle now. *(She hands the bottle to MARGHERITA, who already has her penknife out to open it. FELICE hears a noise and looks up.)* Who's there? *(MARGHERITA freezes.)* Someone is spying on us. *(BENEDETTA steps out from behind the statue. FELICE confronts the stranger.)* What are you doing here?

BENEDETTA: *(Smiling.)* What are *you* doing here? *(MARGHERITA hastily conceals the bottle.)*

MARGHERITA: Men are not allowed in the chapel.

BENEDETTA: I'm not a man. Let me see your bottle... *(MARGHERITA hesitates.)* Come on... *(MARGHERITA produces the bottle. BENEDETTA has her own knife, and she opens it expertly. She smells it and then tastes it.)* Vernaccia... dry, not sweet... San Gimigniano. *(She hands it back to MARGHERITA.)* My father is a vintner. When he dies, I'm going to inherit the business.

FELICE: You're not going to get married?

BENEDETTA: *(Laughing.)* What would I need a wife for? *(To FELICE, taking her measure.)* What's a Mistress of the Novices?

FELICE: *(Eying her coolly.)* It's a position.

BENEDETTA: *(Smiling.)* What kind of position?

MARGHERITA: She teaches the new girls how to sing the chants for the services. We have services six times a day.

13

BENEDETTA: *(To FELICE.)* Six times a day?   Sounds like a prison.

FELICE: Do all the girls of Vellano wear men's clothes?

BENEDETTA: *(Looking at her carefully.)* No. But I like to ride... Don't you?

MARGHERITA: The convent doesn't have horses.

BENEDETTA: *(To FELICE.)* That's too bad...When it's hot in Vellano, I go down to my father's stables... Everyone is asleep, except the horses. I run my hand down the neck of my father's horse, and he lets me lead him. *(To FELICE.)* Have you ever ridden without a saddle?

FELICE: No.

BENEDETTA: *(To FELICE.)* It's like being a centaur. Human on top and animal below. You have to be like that to ride without a saddle. You have to flatten yourself down, your face sideways, pressed hard into the side of his neck. Because, the horse is going to forget that you're there. He becomes too intoxicated with his freedom. When he starts to trot, your legs, without the stirrups, will dangle like broken toys... and when he starts to canter, no matter how tightly you weave your fingers into his mane, you're still going to bruise. Oh, you'll be black and blue by morning... but it's going to be worth it, because you're going to fly...   He's going to teach you to fly... the light flashing across your eyes, the blood roaring in your ears, as he gallops you over those scorched fields, his hooves barely touching the ground...   You'll be traveling faster than your breathing, you'll be in the space between heartbeats. You'll think you're dreaming, or maybe you're dead, only you're not. Because after it's over, his foam will be all over your legs. *(There is a moment of uneasy silence, which is broken by the sound of hysterical laughter offstage. ANGELINA enters laughing and runs through the chapel. She stops in front of the statue of Mary, throws a handful of wildflowers at it, and runs out again. ANGELINA, 18, is a young nun, a victim of massive sexual trauma, who now lives entirely in a dissociated state of consciousness. In her world, she is in Paradise, the beloved daughter of an adoring, omnipotent Mother. BENEDETTA stares after her.)*

MARGHERITA: That's Angelina. *(The noon bells rings.)* She thinks this is Paradise.

BENEDETTA: She must be crazy.

MARGHERITA: She is.

BENEDETTA: *(To FELICE.)* They lock you up with crazy people?

FELICE: We aren't locked up. We can leave if we want to.

BENEDETTA: Why don't you?

MARGHERITA: Because we are going to inherit the kingdom of heaven.

BENEDETTA: When?

MARGHERITA: After we die.

BENEDETTA: *(Laughing.)* I'm want *my* kingdom while I'm still alive.

MARGHERITA: Don't you believe in God?

BENEDETTA: *(To FELICE.)* Show me what he looks like.

MARGHERITA: This is what Mary looks like.

BENEDETTA: *(Walking around the statue.)* A block of wood...?

MARGHERITA: Don't touch her!

BENEDETTA: Why not?

MARGHERITA: It's a sacrilege! You would go to hell...

BENEDETTA: *(To FELICE.)* Is that what *you* believe?

FELICE: *(Evenly.)* Try it and see. (*Her eyes on FELICE, BENEDETTA moves slowly behind the statue and cups her hands erotically over the Virgin's breasts. FELICE holds her gaze. MARGHERITA lunges for her with her penknife. BENEDETTA is too quick for her. She grabs MARGHERITA's wrist and the two girls wrestle for possession of the knife. BENEDETTA's hand is cut. The statue begins to totter, and MARGHERITA screams.)*

Blackout

End of Scene

ACT I

Scene Four

The office of the ABBESS. This scene is happening at the same time as the previous scene. The ABBESS is at her desk. A NUN enters.

ABBESS: Yes?

NUN: There is a visitor to see you.

ABBESS: Who is it?

NUN: A woman named Midea Carlini. She says she has come about her daughter.

ABBESS: Show her in. *(The NUN exits and MIDEA enters.)*

MIDEA: Reverend Mother... *(The ABBESS motions her to a chair, but MIDEA remains standing.)*

ABBESS: You've come about your daughter?

MIDEA: Yes, Reverend Mother.

ABBESS: And are you from Pescia?

MIDEA: *(Lying.)* Yes.

ABBESS: "Carlini"... I don't recognize the name. *(A beat.)* What is your family's business?

MIDEA: My husband is a vintner.

ABBESS: I know all the vintners in Pescia. *(A tense silence.)*

MIDEA: *(Embarrassed.)* We are from Vellano.

ABBESS: Ah.

17

MIDEA: I was afraid you would only take girls from Pescia.

ABBESS: That's true… and we turn away two out of every three girls who apply. *(Pause.)* Do you have any relatives here at the Congregation of the Mother of God? *(MIDEA shakes her head. Pause.)* Have you tried Santa Maria Nuova?

MIDEA: They only accept girls whose fathers were eligible for public office in Pescia.

ABBESS: *(Nodding.)* And Santa Chiara?

MIDEA: They wanted four hundred scudi.

ABBESS: I think San Michele might be able to help you.

MIDEA: They said they were full. *(The ABBESS begins to turn away.)* Please, Reverend Mother… They said this was not an official convent yet and that you would still have room.

ABBESS: You would still have to provide a dowry.

MIDEA: How much?

ABBESS: One hundred and sixty scudi.

MIDEA: *(Eagerly.)* I have a hundred … here… *(Taking out her money. The ABBESS tries to dissuade her.)* And I can get the rest.. My husband makes eight hundred scudi a year.

ABBESS: *(Smiling.)* Some of the girls here have fathers worth ten thousand scudi.

MIDEA: Ten thousand!

ABBESS: I'm sorry, but I can't take a girl from Vellano.

MIDEA: Why?

ABBESS: Because the people here have a great prejudice against mountain people.

MIDEA: What kind of prejudice?

ABBESS: They believe that you have traffic with the devil. *(The ABBESS is turned away from MIDEA when she says this. MIDEA starts.)* People always believe the devil is somewhere else. *(Turning back to face MIDEA.)* Your daughter would not fit in.

MIDEA: *(Desperate.)* Take her as a servant, then… a "conversa"—

ABBESS: Our "conversa" come from the servant class.

MIDEA: Then let her teach. Benedetta knows how to read and write—She knows Latin!

ABBESS: Do the girls of Vellano go to school?

MIDEA: *(Embarrassed.)* No… My husband… He taught her. He… takes her into the fields… and he teaches her.

ABBESS: No, I'm sorry. It wouldn't work.

MIDEA: *(Kneeling.)* Please, Reverend Mother!

ABBESS: Get your daughter on the waiting list for San Michele. They'll have an opening in a year or two—

MIDEA: *(Hysterical.)* No! *(The ABBESS turns.)* It will be too late! *(Looking up in anguish.)* Mother, have pity on me. *(She looks down in an agony of shame.)* My daughter… she has begun to bleed. *(There is a long silence, as the Abbess takes in the implications of MIDEA's words. The silence is broken by the sound of MARGHERITA's scream from the end of the previous scene. The ABBESS rises quickly and runs out. MIDEA follows.)*

Blackout

End of Scene

ACT I

Scene 5

The chapel. The statue has just fallen and the girls are still wrestling. MIDEA and the ABBESS enter, running.

MIDEA: Benedetta! *Cavolo!* What have you done? *(BENEDETTA conceals the knife wound on her hand.)*

MARGHERITA: She touched the statue!

MIDEA: *Disgraziata! (MIDEA slaps her daughter, hard, across her face. She starts to hit her again.)*

ABBESS: *(Stepping between them.)* Stop!

MARGHERITA: *(To the ABBESS.)* She knocked it over! I tried to stop her!

MIDEA: *(Reaching around the ABBESS.)* Diablo! Devil child!

MARGHERITA: Mother Pagni—

ABBESS: All right, Margherita! *(Turning to MIDEA.)* Senora...this is this your daughter?

MIDEA: *(To BENEDETTA.) Puttana!* She is her *father's* daughter! *(To the ABBESS.)* You see how it is? Look at her! She is wild... like an animal! *(Intrigued, the ABBESS turns to BENEDETTA.)*

ABBESS: Why are you wearing men's clothes?

MIDEA: Aiee! *Puttana! (She spits.)* She is a freak! A monster! She does it to punish her mother for the sin of giving birth—

ABBESS: *(Studying BENEDETTA.)* Do you dress like that, because of men... so they won't see you as a woman?

BENEDETTA: *(Studying the ABBESS.)* They can see me any way they like. *(Just then FATHER RICORDATI enters.)*

RICORDATI: What is going on? *(Seeing the fallen statue, he crosses himself.)* Holy Mother of God! Who has committed this sacrilege? Margherita!

MARGHERITA: It wasn't me!

RICORDATI: Don't lie to me...

ABBESS: Father, we have a visitor...

RICORDATI: *(Seeing BENEDETTA.)* What! A young man in the chapel of the Congregation of the Mother of God? *(Turning to the ABBESS.)* Have you lost your mind, Piera?

ABBESS: She's a woman, Father—

RICORDATI: *(Cutting her off.)* This is what comes of your open policies. I'm going to report this to the Provost...! *(Suddenly BENEDETTA is seized by a convulsion. She drops to her knees with a cry. They all turn to look at her. She doesn't move.)* What is this?

BENEDETTA: *(Transfixed.)* The light... the light...

RICORDATI: What light?

BENEDETTA: It blinds me!

RICORDATI: What light?

MIDEA: Oh, the little actress!

RICORDATI: *(To BENEDETTA.)* You see a light?

MIDEA: *(Disgusted.)* She is play-acting! Such a little liar—

RICORDATI: *(To MIDEA.)* Silence! *(To BENEDETTA.)* Tell us what you see, child.

BENEDETTA: I see a great light… and there's a voice..

RICORDATI: And what does the voice say?

BENEDETTA: *(Rising as if in a trance, and speaking with a different voice.)* "Rejoice ye with Jerusalem—"

RICORDATI: Isaiah! She quotes the prophet Isaiah! *Mirabile dictu!* *(Crossing himself.)*

BENEDETTA: "… That ye may suck, and be satisfied with the breasts of her consolations—"

MIDEA: *(Muttering.)* Porca puttana!

RICORDATI: *(To FELICE and MARGHERITA.)* Kneel! Kneel down! We are in the presence of the Holy Spirit! *(They kneel.)*

BENEDETTA: "…and as one whom his mother comforteth, so will I comfort you; and ye shall be comforted…" *(She convulses again and falls prostrate.)*

RICORDATI: Child! *(BENEDETTA moans and opens her eyes.)*

BENEDETTA: Am I dead?

MIDEA: Oh, you will be when I get you home!

RICORDATI: *(Extremely excited.)* This is a sign, Piera! This is a sign of God's favor to your Congregation! The girl must stay!

MIDEA: *(Shocked.)* What? *(Crossing herself, she throws herself at RICORDATI's feet and tries to kiss his hands.)* Oh! *Madra de Dio! Grazi! Grazi! Grazi!*

ABBESS: *(Slowly, to BENEDETTA.)* Benedetta, would you like to stay with us?

RICORDATI: *(Cutting in, to BENEDETTA.)* My child, God has chosen you as a vessel for His truth—and, through your lips—the ignorant, untutored lips of the meanest of God's creatures, He has caused the words of the mighty prophet Isaiah to be heard. You will stay with us, for, truly, "blessed art thou among women..."

MARGUERITE: But, Uncle, she touched the statue!

BENEDETTA: *(Quickly, eyes downcast.)* It's true. I touched it.

RICORDATI: *(Gently, to BENEDETTA.)* And why did you touch it, my child?

MARGHERITA: She said it was only a block of wood!

RICORDATI: *You* are the block of wood!

BENEDETTA: I thought I saw drops of blood falling like tears from the eyes of the Blessed Mother...

RICORDATI: *(Excited.)* Margherita!—and you, Felice—help her! Set the statue up again. *(They obey. The front of the statue is smeared with blood. RICORDATI crosses himself in ecstasies.)* Blood! This is a great sign... a great sign of God's favor!

MARGHERITA: But she—

RICORDATI: Margherita! Go and spend the day in prayer for your sins. And you, too, Felice. *(They exit.)* And I shall offer my prayers of gratitude. *(He exits.)*

MIDEA: *(To the ABBESS.)* Grazi... grazi... *(MIDEA turns to go.)*

ABBESS: Senora Carlini... *(MIDEA turns back.)* Don't you wish to say good-bye to your daughter?

MIDEA: My daughter? *(Turning to BENEDETTA.)* From now on, she—*(Indicating the statue.)* ... shall be your mother! *(She exits. For a moment, the ABBESS and BENEDETTA look at each other.)*

ABBESS: *(Observing coolly.)* It appears you have cut your hand…

BENEDETTA: *(Watching her.)* Yes.

ABBESS: … and it's bleeding. *(BENEDETTA does not respond.)* I understand that your father has taught you to read and to write…

BENEDETTA: Among other things.

ABBESS: It appears you are familiar enough with the Scriptures to quote them? *(BENEDETTA does not respond.)* Let me speak plainly to you, Benedetta. I am the Abbess here. I have organized this Congregation—and it is a "congregation," not a convent. I have organized this with my own money, because I want it to be a place of refuge and sanctuary for women who don't want to marry. I retain the right to accept or refuse the women, and I can also send them away. There are no miracles here, except the ordinary miracle of healing that happens when women are protected and loved. The only tears that are shed here are our own, for our lives, for our losses. The only blood that flows is the natural blood of our own bodies as they renew themselves monthly. The only voices that are heard here are our own, which are never heard or honored outside the walls like ours. And the only grace to be displayed here is the grace of tolerance and forgiveness that we extend to ourselves and to our wounded sisters. Do you understand me?

BENEDETTA: Yes.

ABBESS: Good. *(She turns to go.)*

BENEDETTA: And may *I* speak plainly? *(The ABBESS turns back.)* Don't ever talk to me like I'm a child, because I'm not. I never was. Don't ever talk to me like I'm a social inferior, because I'm your equal, and possibly your better. Do you understand?

ABBESS: You're speaking very clearly.

BENEDETTA: And don't ever lie to me. Ever. *(The two women look at each other.)*

Blackout

End of Scene

ACT I

Scene 6

Two years later, moving day at the Congregation of the Mother of God, and the courtyard is piled with crates and bundles. It's a sunny spring morning, Annunciation Day, March 25, 1618. MAURA, one of the older "conversa," or convent servants, is inventorying a stack of crates. MAURA is a dependable worker and deeply religious woman, loyal to the Abbess. MEA enters carrying a crate. BARTHOLMEA CRIVELLI, or "MEA," is a young conversa, the most recent member of the convent. She, like Angelica, is a survivor of sexual abuse. MEA embraces every aspect of convent life with enthusiasm.

MAURA: *(Flustered.)* Here! Mea! Bring that crate over here! We don't want the cooking pots mixed up with the gardening tools... Look at this mess! It's going to take me weeks to sort things out after we move to the new convent! *(Calling to MEA.)* And hurry! We've got to get everything out to the courtyard by noon. That's when the procession begins. And you know, once we all leave here, that's it. There's no looking back. We've got to take everything today. *(MEA lugs the crate over for her inspection.)* Wait! What is this? I don't remember—

MEA: These are the serving bowls. You asked me to pack them after I finished with the pots...

MAURA: *(Upset.)* Then where are the pots?

MEA: *(Pointing to a crate on the stack.)* Here. I finished with them this morning.

MAURA: Oh... And what about this? *(Pointing to a small crate.)*

MEA: Oh, those are the herbs. I saw them hanging in the rafters, and I thought you might have forgotten them. I wrapped them in the aprons and packed them separately so they wouldn't get crushed.

26

MAURA: *(Striking her forehead.)* This move will be the death of me! And look at you... You've only been here, what, a few weeks...?

MEA: I've been here for two months and five days exactly.

MAURA: Well, you've settled right into the routine here, haven't you?

MEA: I love it.

MAURA: Even the bells?

MEA: *Especially* the bells! I always know where I should be and what I should be doing.

MAURA: But doesn't that bother you... having to get up in the dead of night?

MEA: Oh, I'm usually up anyway.

MAURA: You are?

MEA: *(Embarrassed.)* I don't sleep very well at night.

MAURA: Yes, well, none of us do—thanks to those bells.

MEA: But they remind us to pray.

MAURA: Don't they? And what do you think we're praying for? That their little clappers drop off, that's what! *(Just then MARGHERITA enters.)*

MARGHERITA: Mea! Mea! I've been looking everywhere for you! *(MEA turns around.)* Go up to my room and bring down my trunk!

MAURA: Whoa, there, Missy! Mea is helping me with packing up the refectory.

MARGHERITA: But I need her to help me with my trunk!

MAURA: Mea, go pack the cutlery—

MEA: It's packed.

MARGHERITA: See? She can help me—

MAURA: *(Ignoring MARGHERITA.)* And the baking pans?

MEA: In with the pots… *(She indicates the crate with the pots.)*

MARGHERITA: *(Exasperated.)* Maura…!

MAURA: *(To MEA.)* Then go help Caterina dig up the tomato plants. *(MEA exits. MAURA turns to MARGHERITA.)* Now, you listen to me, Margherita D'Iptolito Ricordati, Mea is a conversa. She works with me in the kitchen. She's not your personal servant. And just because your uncle is the confessor for this congregation, don't go thinking you can order her around.

MARGHERITA: If you let me help you, I will give you my purple slippers. You could wear them in the procession today—when the whole convent parades through the streets of Pescia and over the bridge to the new convent. Everyone would see them..

MAURA: Sandals were good enough for my savior, and they're good enough for me! *(She exits. CRISTINA has entered and been listening. CRISTINA is a nun about MARGHERITA's age. She has keen powers of observation and a quick wit.)*

CRISTINA: Hey, have you heard the news? *(FELICE GUERRINI and CECILIA BIANCHI enter. FELICE has her arms around CECILIA, her partner. CECILIA is a nervous, deeply conservative young woman, very traditionally beautiful. Like FELICE, she is from an aristocratic family.)*

CECILIA: What news?

CRISTINA: That they're going to enclose us after the move today.

FELICE: *(Behind her.)* No, they're not.

CRISTINA: *(Challenging her.)* Then why are there grates on all the windows and doors?

MARGHERITA: Who told you that?

CRISTINA: Caterina. Her brother is one of the plasterers. *(MEA enters carrying a box of plants.)* Mea! *(MEA turns.)* You work with Caterina in the kitchen, don't you?

MEA: Yes.

CRISTINA: Did she tell you about the grates?

MEA: No… Do I need to pack them? *(They laugh.)*

MARGHERITA: We're talking about the grates at the new convent. They're going to enclose us.

FELICE: No, they're not.

MEA: What does that mean?

CRISTINA: It means you're going to be a prisoner, Mea. You'll never be able to leave. You'll have to talk to all your visitors through the little holes in the grate, and you'll never be able to get away, no matter how much you hate it… Ever!

MEA: *(Terrified.)* No!

FELICE: *(To CRISTINA.)* Stop scaring her. *(To MEA.)* It's not true.

MEA: I'm not going to be a prisoner?

FELICE: No. Mother Pagni will never turn us over to the Church.

CRISTINA: But what if she dies?

FELICE: Then I will become the new Abbess—

MEA: But she's not going to die!

CRISTINA: Yes, she is.

MEA: No!

FELICE: Stop it, Cristina! *(To MEA.)* She's not going to die.

CRISTINA: *(To FELICE.)* How do you know? She has a bad heart.

MEA: *(In tears.)* No! She has a good heart! Mother Pagni took me in when none of the other convents would... She has a good heart! *(FELICE puts her arms around MEA to comfort her.)*

CRISTINA: *(Defensively.)* She had a stroke three years ago.

CECILIA: *(Defending FELICE and MEA.)* But she hasn't had any problems since.

CRISTINA: *(Surprised to hear CECILIA speak, she baits her.)* And I wonder what miracle could have healed her? Maybe you can tell us, Cecilia... Didn't your heart undergo some kind of miraculous transformation...

CECILIA: What are you talking about?

CRISTINA: Well... let's see... When you first came here, you were crying all the time and wanting to go home, but then all of a sudden, you started wearing your finest dresses, and putting ribbons in your hair, and singing all the time, just like a little birdy— *(Turning to FELICE.)* Didn't she, Felice? Do you remember? It was just about the time you started spending all your time with her—

FELICE: *(Cutting her off.)* What's your point?

CRISTINA: Well, after Sister Benedetta of the Bleeding Tears came to stay with us, the Abbess started spending all her time with her... and now you say her heart—

30

CECILIA: *(Defensive.)* Benedetta is Mother Pagni's secretary.

CRISTINA: Oh. Is that what you call it...?

MARGHERITA: *(Egging CRISTINA on.)* What would *you* call it?

CRISTINA: "*Peccatum mutum.*" *(MARGHERITA sniggers.)*

MEA: *(Confused, to FELICE.)* What's she laughing at?

CRISTINA: *(To MEA.)* Don't you know what "*peccatum mutum*" means?

MARGHERITA: *(To MEA.)* "The silent sin."

CRISTINA: I don't know what's so silent about it. *(MARGHERITA sniggers again.)*

MEA: *(Upset, to FELICE.)* What are they talking about?

CECILIA: They don't know. They're just stupid.

MARGHERITA: Yes, we do. *(She makes an obscene gesture. CRISTINA laughs. MEA is puzzled.)* Carnal knowledge. *Fornication!*

MEA: No!

MARGHERITA: Yes! My uncle told me about it. They burned two nuns at the stake in Spain!

CECILIA: *(Visibly upset, to FELICE.)* That's not true, is it?

FELICE: We don't have to worry about what they do in Spain.

MARGHERITA: My uncle said that they would burn nuns here if they caught them.

CRISTINA: Well, Father Ricordati would certainly know all about *"peccatum mutum."*

MARGHERITA: What do you mean by that?

CRISTINA: Why do you think they moved him to a *convent? (Just then, FATHER RICORDATI enters.)*

FATHER RICORDATI: Girls! Girls! A little decorum! Have you forgotten what day this is? The day of the blessed Annunciation! Do you think that the Angel Gabriel would have appeared to the Holy Virgin if she had been gossiping in the courtyard with her sisters?

CRISTINA: Father... *(He turns.)* Is it true that the new convent is going to be enclosed?

FATHER RICORDATI: Where did you hear that?

MARGHERITA: They've put grates on all the doors!

FATHER RICORDATI: That was a mistake. Mother Pagni has already ordered them removed. *(The women respond with relief. This antagonizes the priest.)* Although it would be a great blessing. A true penitent cuts her hair with joy, renounces the vanity of fashion with relief, embracing the simplicity of the nun's habit as a protection and a passport on a pilgrim's journey toward humility. Her sacrifices can never compensate for that one supreme sacrifice of the most perfect man who ever walked among the heathen, who ever touched the leper to heal him, who said to the Magdalene—that wretched whore—"Let he who is without sin cast the first stone." *(MEA begins to cry. FATHER RICORDATI is shocked and discomfited by her response.)* There! Yes, that's enough...

MEA: Father...

FATHER RICORDATI: All right... All right...

MEA: *(Throwing herself at his feet.)* Father, I am so wicked!

FATHER RICORDATI: *(Vaguely.)* Yes... Child, we all see... uh, through a glass darkly… as it were…

MEA: *(Hysterical.)* You don't know! I am so wicked!

FATHER RICORDATI: Yes. All right… *(To the other sisters.)* Go! Finish your packing! The procession is at noon… *(The women disperse, except for MEA, who is still clinging to RICORDATI, and MARGHERITA who is watching.)*

MEA: Father—Please! Hear my confession!

FATHER RICORDATI: Not now!

MEA: *(Distraught.)* But I am too sinful to be among you! I am too wicked to be here with the other women! I am more sinful than the Magdalene!

FATHER RICORDATI: *(Shaking her.)* Sister Bartholmea!

MEA: *(Shocked.)* Father?

FATHER RICORDATI: You will remember where you are! Whatever sins you have committed, do not allow them to keep you from performing your duties. Do you understand? *(Pausing.)* You don't want to add disobedience to the inventory, do you?

MEA: No, Father.

FATHER RICORDATI: Then go—! Be about your Father's business!

MEA: Yes, Father. *(Devastated, MEA exits. FATHER RICORDATI starts to exit, but MARGHERITA stops him.)*

MARGHERITA: Uncle… What about Benedetta?

FATHER RICORDATI: What about her?

MARGHERITA: They say she's going to walk in front, with the Abbess.

FATHER RICORDATI: *(Exasperated.)* Then she'll walk in front with the Abbess. Margherita, if you paid more attention to your *own* position—

MARGHERITA: *(Insolent.)* If *you* paid more attention to *your* position, you might not want to have Benedetta in the front.

FATHER RICORDATI: What do you mean?

MARGHERITA: People are saying that Benedetta is the Abbess' "special friend."

FATHER RICORDATI: Where did you hear that?

MARGHERTIA: Everyone is saying it. And if you let her walk in front of the girls who have been here longer than her—

FATHER RICORDATI: All right. All right... Go pack the altar—

MARGHERITA: But that's the conversa's job—

FATHER RICORDATI: The conversa aren't allowed to handle the cross. Go! *(MARGHERITA exits. Disturbed, RICORDATI watches her go.)*

Blackout

End of Scene

ACT I

Scene 7

Lights come up in the Abbess' office, the same day. The ABBESS, sitting at her desk, is packing up the records of the Congregation of the Mother of God. BENEDETTA enters with a sheaf of papers.

ABBESS: Benedetta!

BENEDETTA: Did you look at the figures on the Fucecchio commune? *(She spreads the papers in front of the ABBESS.)* Looking at their yield for the last five years... *(Indicating.)* ... I have projected the net income for the next five... *(Indicating again.)... augmented* by projected profits from putting an additional twelve acres under cultivation—

ABBESS: *(Pushing the papers away.)* Oh... no... I'm sorry... The move... all the packing... I forgot all about it... I'm sorry.

BENEDETTA: They're asking seventeen hundred and fifty scudi. That's high, but I think we can recover it in less than three years from the tenants—and that's *without* the additional cultivation—

ABBESS: *(Rising distractedly.)* Oh, Benedetta—look at this! Everything is in crates, and it's going to be chaos once we get into the new buildings. And every girl is going to be complaining to me about something that isn't as good as it was here, and I'm going to be putting out hundreds of little brush fires for the next six months...

BENEDETTA: If we wait that long, the Bianchi's will find out that we've been looking at the property, and they'll raise their offer. We have to act now.

ABBESS: *(Looking at her.)* Next week.

BENEDETTA: Tomorrow. *(The ABBESS hesitates.)* We can close the deal before the Bianchi's have a chance to revise their offer. I can use the relocation of the convent as an excuse. I'll tell them that I have the money to meet their price today, but that, if they make us wait even one day, I can't guarantee that I will have it again for at least a year. *(Smiling.)* They'll take it.

ABBESS: *(Laughing.)* Go ahead…

BENEDETTA: You won't regret it. It's beautiful… up in the foothills overlooking the Pescia River… We can ride out and look at the sunsets. There is a grove of trees, and a creek with waterfalls—

ABBESS: You're impossible!

BENEDETTA: I'm very possible.

ABBESS: Yes… you are. And that's the miracle. *(BENEDETTA smiles. The ABBESS takes her hands.)* Women are kept so cramped—so ignorant, and so afraid of our own shadows. When we get to the new convent, I want you to teach the other women what you know about money. I actually want each sister to be given some portion of the convent assets to manage. I used to envision the Congregation as just a refuge, a place of sanctuary, but you have changed all that, because you are very possible. *(Suddenly there is knock on the door.)*

FATHER RICORDATI: *(Offstage.)* Piera… !

ABBESS: *(With a start.)* Father Ricordati! Yes… Come in! *(BENEDETTA crosses quickly away from the ABBESS. He enters.)* Father—

BENEDETTA: *(Lowering her head.)* Father.

FATHER RICORDATI: Sister Benedetta.

ABBESS: As you can see, Father, we're very busy packing…

FATHER RICORDATI: I'm afraid this can't wait.

36

ABBESS: Yes... Benedetta... Can you wait in the chapel? *(BENEDETTA exits and the ABBESS turns to the priest.)* Yes?

FATHER RICORDATI: It's about... about the arrangements for the procession... May I see them?

ABBESS: *(Puzzled.)* I didn't feel it necessary to write it down.

FATHER RICORDATI: I thought that might be the case, and so I have taken the liberty myself... *(He hands her a paper with a list of names. Surprised, she takes it and looks at it.)*

ABBESS: I want Sister Benedetta at the front. She and Sister Felice will walk together, after me.

FATHER RICORDATI: Sister Benedetta has only recently joined us. She will walk with the other new girls, at the back.

ABBESS: But what about Sister Felice? She has only been here a year longer than Benedetta, and you have put *her* at the head of the line.

FATHER RICORDATI: There are other, compelling reasons for the daughter of Giovanni Guerrini to be at the front.

ABBESS: Just as there are other, compelling reasons for my assistant to be at the front. *(The two look at each other.)*

FATHER RICORDATI: I have never interfered in your decisions—

ABBESS: Nor would I expect you to, as we are not an official convent. *(Annoyed.)* This whole procession business was never my idea in the first place. Parading us through the town and over that damned bridge...

FATHER RICORDATI: *(With dignity.)* The reputation of the Congregation can only be enhanced by its association with the miracle.

ABBESS: *(Heatedly.)* I don't want *any* association with so-called miracles—

FATHER RICORDATI: But what about the tears on the statue? That blood was real! You saw it yourself!

ABBESS: In a convent of several dozen women, Father, we are very accustomed to the sight of blood. *(He is shocked. She turns away.)* Whatever the truth behind that day, the statue has not wept or bled since—nor do I expect that it will. And as far as Benedetta—

FATHER RICORDATI: *(Cutting in.)* Exactly! That girl was a chosen vessel of the Lord, and, by making her your assistant—

ABBESS: *(Turning back to him.)* By making her my assistant, I have effectively given her scope for her talents. Did you know that we shall be entirely self-sufficient within the next ten years?

FATHER RICORDATI: Careful, Piera!

ABBESS: Careful! Careful! We shall all die of being too careful! Pricked to death by the thousand little stitches of our uselessly embroidered lives! Do you hear me? And this girl, Benedetta—She is gifted! I've never seen such a brilliantly analytical mind—such ambition—such an appetite for life, Father! And you would put her at the back of the line—

FATHER RICORDATI: She's a newcomer! That's the place for newcomers!

ABBESS: If you try to put that girl in back, you will force her to find a way to the front. She is different from the others—feral, where the others have been domesticated.

FATHER RICORDATI: You appear to be very attached to the girl.

ABBESS: *(Indignant.)* Sister Benedetta is my assistant, Father. We *work* together.

FATHER RICORDATI: People will talk.

ABBESS: And just what could they say?

FATHER RICORDATI: What could they say? *(He begins to pace.)* What could they say about a priest who took an interest in the spiritual welfare of the young men—boys, really—of his parish, those unfathered sons whose only caress had been a slap, or a kick, whose only words of paternal counsel had been cruel mockery and ridicule, whose every instinct toward higher sentiment had been choked and brutalized at every turn? What could they say about a priest, not much older than his charges, who was longing to offer them the kind of tender embrace they never had—seeing, as you do with Sister Benedetta—the shining promise in them, a promise that, without cultivation, would like the proverbial seed that fell by the wayside, be devoured by predation, or wither from stony neglect, or else be choked by the gross sensualism and selfish hedonism of their more brutish brothers? What could they say about a priest who took his Lord's injunction seriously to "suffer the children come unto me"—whose calling, whose ministry was to these stray lambs... these beautiful boys? They could say—and they *did* say—that this man was a corrupter of youth—

ABBESS: *(Alarmed.)* Father, what are you telling me?

FATHER RICORDATI: *(Looking at her.)* I am telling you that I was accused of sodomy, and because of that, I lost my position in the Church and was sent to a community of nothing but women, to be your confessor. *(The ABBESS sits.)* They hated me without a cause... But I was lucky. The Church spared me the Inquisition... this time. But they told me, one more infraction, and I will be tried for the former charges in addition to the new, found guilty and sentenced to death at the stake. *(He picks up the list and hands it to the ABBESS.)* I give you this for your own good, and I advise you in the strongest possible terms to see to it that it is implemented when those girls get ready to cross over that bridge today. *(He exits. The ABBESS, profoundly disturbed, picks up the list.)*

Blackout

End of Scene

Act I

Scene 8

The interior of the chapel. MARGHERITA is attempting to wrap the cross in an altar cloth. CRISTINA enters.

CRISTINA: What? Stealing the Holy Cross?

MARGHERITA: *(Defensively.)* No…! My uncle told me to pack it. *(She tries to bundle it in an altar cloth with the candlesticks.)*

CRISTINA: Don't wrap the candlesticks in the altar cloth! You'll get wax on it!

MARGHERITA: Well, what am I supposed to use?

CRISTINA: Well, look around! Here… *(She opens a chest.)* Here… use this rag… *(She hands MARGHERITA a stained, coarse-looking garment.)*

MARGHERITA: It's got blood on it! *(Suddenly MAURA enters.)*

MAURA: What are you girls doing?

MARGHERITA: Look… It's got blood on it!

MAURA: *(Alarmed.)* Where did you get those?

MARGHERITA: The chest behind the altar.

CRISTINA: We needed something to wrap the altar candles—

MAURA: That chest belongs to Father Ricordati! He brought it with him from his monastery and you're not be poking around in it! *(CRISTINA immediately crosses to it.)*

CRISTINA: They're shirts!

MAURA: Get out of there! *(She rushes toward CRISTINA, but MARGHERITA is already pulling another item out of the chest.)*

MARGHERITA: What's this? Look! There are dozens of them—

MAURA: Stop it! Stop it right now! You don't know what you're doing!

CRISTINA: It looks like some kind of whip…

MAURA: And if Father Ricordati could see the two of you rummaging like a pair of magpies—

MARGHERITA: It's so short! It would never reach the backside of a horse.

MAURA: It's long enough to reach the backside of an ass. *(She grabs the whip and swats MARGHERITA.)*

MARGHERITA: Ouch!

CRISTINA: Maura, what are these? And why are these shirts all stiff with dried blood?

MARGHERITA: If you don't tell us, we'll ask my uncle and if he gets mad, we'll say it was your fault we found them.

MAURA: *(Angry.)* If this was a real convent and you were real Christians, you wouldn't be needing to ask. *(She grabs the shirt from CRISTINA, but soon as she does that, they both grab shirts and whips from the open trunk.)* You little heathens! *(The girls wait.)* It's not a whip. It's called a discipline. It's used for penitence.

CRISTINA: *(She smacks MARGHERITA. MAURA takes it.)* So what about the shirts?

MAURA: They're for penitence, too.

MARGHERITA: They stink. *(CRISTINA laughs.)*

41

CRISTINA: They're made from goat hair, which is why they smell... isn't that right, Maura?

MAURA: *(Disgusted.)* These are for the reunciates who have taken vows to consecrate their lives to the service of our Lord. They use the discipline to mortify the flesh and sanctify the spirit. Here... you help me move this to the courtyard. *(The three of them exit. After a moment, BENEDETTA enters. She walks up to the statue of Mary. She pauses and then thoughtfully reaches out and touches the statue's breasts. The ABBESS appears.)*

ABBESS: Benedetta—

BENEDETTA: *(Turning quickly.)* Mother...

ABBESS: Father Ricordati has asked me to change the order of the procession... *(A nervous pause.)* You'll be in the back with the other girls who have only been here for a few years.

BENEDETTA: What does *he* have to do with it? You're the *Abbess*. This is *your* Congregation! *(A beat.)* What about Felice?

ABBESS: *(Looking away.)* The Guerrini's have donated the new chapel—

BENEDETTA: No!

ABBESS: ... and it's still only half-finished—

BENEDETTA: I can pay for that chapel in five months! Just let me buy that Fucecchio commune and—

ABBESS: ... *and* they pay a sizable percentage of our annual operating expenses—

BENEDETTA: In five years, we won't need their money! We'll be completely self-supporting!

ABBESS: But we need it now—

BENEDETTA: Then let me get a loan against the new property—

ABBESS: Benedetta! Even if we bought all the vineyards in Pescia, we would still need peasants to work in them, and we would still need vintners to buy our grapes, and they would still need merchants to vend their wines. If we insult the Guerrini's, there will not be anyone in Pescia who will buy from us or sell to us or work for us. That is a fact of life. We need the patronage of these powerful families.

BENEDETTA: I can't believe you put Felice in the front and me in the back. After all the work I've done for you...

ABBESS: Benedetta, I had to.

BENEDETTA: No, you didn't *have* to. "Have to" is when your arm is twisted around your back until you feel the bones come out of the socket. "Have to" is when someone wraps his hands around your throat and squeezes it until you can't breathe. You didn't *have* to put me in the back. You *wanted* to.

ABBESS: *(Cutting her off.)* It was for the sake of the convent—

BENEDETTA: Everyone is going to see how disrespected I am—at the back of the line!

ABBESS: Benedetta—

BENEDETTA: I'm grateful to you.

ABBESS: Benedetta

BENEDETTA: I am. For reminding me of my place. For reminding me that, even with your patronage, I am still at the back of the line. For reminding me that, if anything were to happen to you, I would be nothing but a convent servant, a conversa!

ABBESS: No!

BENEDETTA: Yes! I would be washing the underwear of Felice and her crowd! No money, no family connections. If you were to die, Piera, I would have nothing. Nothing! I've been a fool. I'm leaving. *(She turns to go.)*

ABBESS: Benedetta—wait! There's another reason... *(Pause.)* Father Ricordati is afraid—

BENEDETTA: Afraid of what?

ABBESS: Of... rumors... *(BENEDETTA looks at her.)* Rumors about us... about you and me... That I might be... *(She struggles to find the right word.)* ... favoring you.

BENEDETTA: I should hope you would. I've doubled your assets—

ABBESS: No—that we might be... *(In an agony of humiliation.)* ... in love.

BENEDETTA: *(Simply.)* Aren't we?

ABBESS: *(Startled.)* What?

BENEDETTA: Piera! *(She freezes.)* Oh, come on! Do you think I didn't see it in your eyes that first day in the chapel? Of course, we're in love.

ABBESS: Of course, we're not!

BENEDETTA: *(Crossing next to her.)* Do you remember what I said to you? "Don't ever lie to me..." *(Slowly she puts her arms around the ABBESS's waist.)*

ABBESS: No...

BENEDETTA: *(Teasingly.)* "Don't ever lie to me..." *(Overwhelmed, the ABBESS does not respond. BENEDETTA releases her.)* Do you know why Eve was thrown out of Paradise? It wasn't for eating the apple. It was because she was born of Adam's rib… from a man's *rib*! Think of it, Piera… She never knew the ecstasy of putting her lips around the soft nipple of another woman, to feel it harden as she sucked gently, insistently, those fragrant, engorged breasts. Eve was born of Adam's rib, but we—*we*— came from a woman's womb, from her warm belly, from inside of her…Inside of our goddess! When she was well-fed, we were satisfied. When she was hungry, we suffered with her. When she was frightened, our heart raced in time with hers, and when she was flooded with ecstasy, we shared her bliss—

ABBESS: Benedetta—

BENEDETTA: We all—all!—came through a woman's legs. All of us! Her head thrown back—screaming, her back arching in labor, as she shoved us down that tight, muscle-ribbed passage of life and death… Our first smells—*everyone's* first smells!—the rich, acrid smell of her damp vulva, our first touch—*everyone's* first touch!— the tangled wiry hairs around her labia. Blood, Piera… Blood flowing everywhere, like a spilt secret between us, her body bleeding like a broken promise, like a broken heart!—Blood, sweet, thick, almost black, bathing our face, in our eyes, filling our virgin nostrils. A woman's body… a woman's mysteries… That's what all these cathedrals, all these rituals are about. These men… they can't create life! All they can do is worship death.

ABBESS: *(Pulling away.)* We can't—

BENEDETTA: This is the garden, Piera. This is the holy of holies… This is the fruit of the tree of life that their God would keep all to himself, but we *can* eat of it… *(She begins to kiss her.)*

ABBESS: No… no…

BENEDETTA: Take… eat… *(The ABBESS closes her eyes. BENEDETTA puts her hands over the ABBESS' breasts. Suddenly the ABBESS gasps. She begins to struggle. BENEDETTA, not understanding that her distress is physical, tightens her hold.)*

ABBESS: My heart… my heart…!

BENEDETTA: *(With passion.)* *My* heart! My own! My sacred heart... *(Suddenly the ABBESS slumps to the floor. BENEDETTA freezes in horror.)*

ABBESS: *(Reaching up to her.)* Benedetta...!

BENEDETTA: No! *(The ABBESS is struggling for breath. She dies.)* No! No! *(BENEDETTA embraces the ABBESS' body. Suddenly, the sound of ANGELINA's laughter is heard offstage.)*

Blackout

End of Act I

Act I

Scene 9

An area to the side of the bridge over the Pescia River. It is late afternoon of the same day—March 25, 1618. There is a gathering of townspeople, all lined up to watch the procession of nuns from the Congregation of the Mother of God. CECCHI stands in the front of the crowd. FATHER RICORDATI enters. (This scene can be performed without the crowd.)

RICORDATI: *(Pushing his way through the crowd.)* Excuse me! Excuse me…! Provost! Provost Cecchi! *(CECCHI turns.)* Are they here? Have I missed it?

CECCHI: *(Turning.)* What?

RICORDATI: Have the girls crossed over the bridge yet?

CECCHI: No.

RICORDATI: *(Catching his breath.)* Oh, good! I believe that I have made the right decision, and that Mother Piera would not have wanted her death to prevent the procession to the new convent… Don't you agree, Provost?

CECCHI: *(Dryly.)* So… are you the new Abbess, "Mother" Ricordati?

RICORDATI: *(Stiffly.)* I am *providing guidance* until the nuns can hold an election.

CECCHI: And when will that be?

RICORDATI: As soon as they are in the new buildings… Oh..! Here they come! They're on the bridge!

CECCHI: And look… there's your future superior in the front of the line… Felice Guerini. *(The sound of distant chanting. The crowd freezes. Suddenly the chanting stops.)*

RICORDATI: What? What is it? They've stopped!

CECCHI: They seem to be turning around.

RICORDATI: Turning around? What?

CECCHI: Calm down, Father. They're just turning to look at something. There's something going on at the back of the line.

RICORDATI: What? What is it?

CECCHI: There's a girl who has fallen.

RICORDATI: Fallen?

CECCHI: No, wait—She hasn't fallen… She's on her knees. It appears that she's praying…

RICORDATI: *(His excitement mounting.)* Let me see! *(He shoves his way to the front of the crowd.)* Where? It's Benedetta! *(To CECCHI.)* Benedetta Carlini. *(Turning back.)* Right in the middle of the bridge! That's the spot! *(Turning with excitement to CECCHI.)* That's where the Virgin appeared! *(To the crowd who has turned to him.)* I was there! I saw it! *(RICORDATI looks toward the bridge again.)* She's rising! She's raising her arms… Oh! Holy Mother of God! *(He crosses himself. The crowd responds with awe.)*

CECCHI: *(Blocked by the crowd.)* What is it? Ricordati, what the hell is it?

RICORDATI: Oh, Sweet Mother of God… *(Crossing himself again.)* Twice in the same place…

CECCHI: *What is it?*

RICORDATI: *(Ecstatic, he turns slowly to CECCHI, opening his hands.)* It's her hands… Benedetta's hands…

CECCHI: *(Annoyed.)* What about her hands?

RICORDATI: *(Turning to CECCHI.)* They're bleeding…! She has the stigmata! *(The townspeople kneel in awe. RICORDATI crosses himself again and kneels. CECCHI remains standing.)*

Blackout

End of Scene

Act II

Scene 1

The interior of the new chapel, which is still under construction. It is April 25, 1618, exactly one month after the procession over the bridge. The statue of Mary, Mother of God, from the old convent has been relocated to the new chapel. CECILIA enters the chapel. The sound of hammering is heard offstage. CECILIA genuflects, crosses herself, and kneels to pray. FELICE enters, looking for her.

FELICE: Cecilia! *(CECILIA slumps down in the pew so as not to be seen.)* Cecilia! *(FELICE sees her and starts to cross towards her.)*

CECILIA: No! Go away! I'm praying. *(FELICE has slid into the same pew and starts to touch CECILIA's shoulder.)*

FELICE: Come here… *(She attempts to kiss her.)*

CECILIA: *(Reacting violently.)* Stop it!

FELICE: *(Trying to touch her again.)* What's the matter?

CECILIA: Stop it! Don't touch me! Listen! Listen to that! *(Sound of hammering.)*

FELICE: The carpenters are taking down the rest of the grates.

CECILIA: No, they're not! They're putting them back up! I saw them! You lied to me. You promised me that you would be the abbess when Mother Pagni died. You said we would be safe. You swore that we wouldn't be enclosed! But now Benedetta has the stigmata and she has been elected abbess, and they're putting the grates back on, and we're going to be enclosed, and you are never going to touch me again.

FELICE: I didn't lie to you.

CECILIA: You're not the abbess.

48

FELICE: No, but I'm going to be. *(CECILIA looks at her.)* Benedetta's little performance on the bridge a month ago was very clever. And her timing was perfect. But it takes more than a little bit of blood to become an abbess, as I think Benedetta knows. Why do you think no one has seen her since the election?

CECILIA: She's doing a retreat. She said she was devoting a month to fasting and prayer.

FELICE: Ceci, she's *hiding. (CECILIA lets FELICE play with her hair.)* This retreat is the only way she knows to buy time for herself, but it's not going to work. Margherita has already caught her pricking holes in her hands with a needle and sneaking food from the refectory at night.

CECILIA: Really?

FELICE: Of course. She can't keep it up. I've already spoken to Father Ricordati, and he has promised me that he would respond publicly to my accusations this morning, before the service. He's going to expose Benedetta, and then I'll be the abbess, and those grates are going to come off the doors and windows for good—and I haven't lied to you. Kiss me.

CECILIA: But what if Benedetta finds out it was you?

FELICE: She can't hurt me. From now on, she's going to be just another convent servant…*(FELICE smiles.)* … *if* she decides to stay. *(She kisses CECILIA. Suddenly MARGHERITA bursts in.)*

MARGHERITA: Felice! *(CECILIA jumps back.)*

FELICE: What is it?

MARGHERITA: You didn't tell my uncle it was me, did you? You didn't tell him I was the one who's been spying on Benedetta—

FELICE: Of course not. All Father Ricordati knows is that one of the nuns has observed Benedetta cutting her hands and stealing food. You're not going to get in any trouble.

MARGHERITA: And you're going to make me Mistress of the Cellar?

FELICE: I already told you I would.

CECILIA: The others are coming. *(MARGHERITA crosses quickly to a different pew and kneels as if in prayer. MAURA, MEA, CRISTINA, and the other nuns enter. They are all talking excitedly among themselves. They don't see FELICE and CECILIA.)*

CRISTINA: Of course, they're going to enclose us! What did you think was going to happen when you all voted for Benedetta? You let Father Ricordati bamboozle you with all that crap about stigmata and visions of the Blessed Mother, and now the Church is going to seize all our vineyards and all our pastures and all these expensive, new buildings. They've been wanting to enclose us for years. Mother Pagni was the only one with the balls enough to stand up to them.

MAURA: *Disgraziata!* Disrespecting the dead in the house of God!

CRISTINA: Disrespecting the dead? That's what you did when you elected Benedetta!

MAURA: Mother Pagni chose her for her assistant. It's what Mother Pagni would have wanted! *(There is agreement from the other nuns.)*

CRISTINA: I don't think any of us quite know *what* Mother Pagni wanted with regard to Benedetta, but I do know she wanted these grates off the windows and they're putting them back on this morning!

MEA: But Benedetta has the stigmata!

CRISTINA: Benedetta *bleeds*. Big deal! So do I. So do all of us.

MAURA: *Disgraziata! (The nuns break out in heated argument, shouting at Cristina. Suddenly, RICORDATI enters. The room falls silent.)*

RICORDATI: *(After an impressive, extended pause.)* Today is Good Friday. Today is the day that they took our Lord and crucified him, hammering the nails into his bleeding, open palms, piercing his body through with a lance... yes, they tortured him. And his eyes, blinded by the blood that streamed from the crown of thorns that they had pressed onto his innocent head, his eyes stung by the tears of an unrequited love, looked down on these, his torturers—ungrateful, envious, prideful assassins, and he said, "Father, forgive them... They know not what they do." *(He looks at them and speaks quietly.)* "They know not what they do." *(A long silence, followed by a thunderous accusation.)* And do you—do *you* know what you do? *(Turning dramatically toward the sacristy, he calls:)* Sister Benedetta! *(After a very long pause, BENEDETTA inches her way onto the stage. She is dressed in a hair shirt, her hair is filthy and unkempt, and her face is smeared with ashes. The nuns respond with appropriate awe and horror. Swaying from weakness, BENEDETTA begins to faint, but FATHER RICORDATI rushes forward to support her.)* Let us pray! *(BENEDETTA bows her head, but remains supported by RICORDATI.)* Our Heavenly Father, today an accusation has been made. An accusation against one of your most consecrated handmaidens. *(CECILIA turns to look at FELICE, but FELICE does not register any emotion.)* The accusation has been made that Sister Benedetta took a needle and opened the wounds on her own hands and feet, so that they would bleed in imitation of the wounds of Christ. The accusation has been made that Sister Benedetta Carlini, during her period of Lenten fasting, has been stealing food from the refectory—that she has been taking for her nightly sustenance salami and Cremonese mortadella! *(One of the nuns snickers. At the sound of this, BENEDETTA screams and falls to the floor, writhing in convulsions.)*

BENEDETTA: No... No... My Lord, I am not worthy! *(Suddenly she screams and rises up in the persona of St. Catherine of Siena, speaking in an altered voice.)* Do not be afraid, Benedetta, for I Saint Catherine of Siena shall speak for you. *(FATHER*

RICORDATI crosses himself and kneels in front of her.) I am Saint Catherine of Siena, and I appear to you today through the body of Sister Benedetta, but I am not she. Behold, she is too weak to stand, too exhausted to speak, because, for forty days and forty nights, she has taken no meat. But I come before you in the strength of spirit to declare unto you that God has chosen Benedetta as his beloved, and that the stigmata you see on her hands and feet is real as the holes in our Savior's hands. *(She holds up her hands. The nuns are silent.)* I am come to assure you of the words of our blessed Lord, "This is my beloved Benedetta, in whom I am well pleased." And in electing her Abbess, you have done well, and the Lord has ordained that the Congregation of the Mother of God shall be elevated above all other convents... The Lord has sent me with the tidings that you are to become an enclosed convent—*(Gasps of disbelief, etc.)* ... *and* that, as an enclosed convent, you shall adopt for your guidance, the Rules of the Blessed Saint Augustine—*(This last produces loud cries of protest and astonishment: "The Rules of Saint Augustine!" etc.)* "Henceforth all shall eat from the common table—convent servants and nuns together, there shall be no more personal property, all personal items shall be confiscated, and there shall be no vocal music except plainchant. Finally, every nun shall renounce forever her family's name, and she shall receive a new name, to be assigned by the Abbess. *(She cries out suddenly.)* Felice di Giovanni Guerrini! *(FELICE does not move.)* Felice di Giovanni Guerrini! *(FELICE does not move, although all eyes are on her.)* You have slandered the Beloved of the Lord, and in doing that, you have blasphemed the holy name of the Lord, and you have done this out of pride and love of pomp. Do you confess? *(FELICE does not move.)* I ask you, in the name of God, do you confess? *(FELICE rises and turns to leave.)* Do you confess? *(FELICE turns and faces BENEDETTA. The two women face off for a moment.)*

FELICE: I confess that you are a liar and a terrible actor. *(She turns to leave.)*

BENEDETTA/ST. CATHERINE: Sister Margherita! Sister Bartholmea! Stop her!

FELICE: *(To the two nuns.)* Don't you dare!

BENEDETTA/ST. CATHERINE: Sister Margherita and Sister Bartholmea, it is the will of God that you restrain Sister Felice, for she has a devil. *(There is a commotion among the nuns.)*

FATHER RICORDATI: *(To the two who have turned to him.)* Do as St. Catherine has commanded. *(They seize the astonished FELICE, who attempts to fight them off.)*

BENEDETTA/ST. CATHERINE: Thank you, Father. And now let us all pray. *(RICORDATI and the women kneel and close their eyes. FELICE alone does not.)* Our Father, who art in Heaven, hear our humble prayer today, on behalf of this sister, who is possessed of a demon, a demon that would divide our congregation. Father, help us drive out this demon, for a house divided against itself cannot stand! *(BENEDETTA crosses quickly to the altar and places something on it. FELICE is the only one who watches this. She and BENEDETTA exchange looks.)* Amen. *(The nuns open their eyes and sit.)* Has the Lord sent any of you a sign? *(Silence.)* Have any of you seen a vision or heard a voice from God? *(There is an awkward silence, and suddenly RICORDATI cries out.)*

RICORDATI: There... on the altar! *(He crosses to it, and picks up on object. It is a whip.)*

BENEDETTA/ST. CATHERINE: Behold, the sign! It is the discipline! *(Agitation among the nuns. Turning suddenly to MARGHERITA and MEA.)* Bring the sister forward. *(FELICE tries to throw them off, but suddenly other nuns have joined to restrain her. CECILIA is terrified. FELICE is brought before BENEDETTA.)* Sister Felice, it is the will of God that you renounce your position as Mistress of the Novices and work as a convent servant. Do you accept this as your penance for the sin of pride and for the salvation of your soul?

FELICE: You won't get away with this, Benedetta. My father will have you put in jail.

BENEDETTA/ST. CATHERINE: Sister Bartholmea, remove Sister Felice's scapular. *(She hesitates.)*

FELICE: She wouldn't dare.

BENEDETTA/ST. CATHERINE: Sister Bartholmea, will you defy the commands of St. Catherine of Siena? *(MEA looks at FATHER RICORDATI, who responds with a slight nod. She removes the scapular.)* Sister Margherita, you will apply the discipline to Sister Felice. *(MARGHERITA hesitates. FELICE looks at her.)* This is for the salvation of her soul... Every lash of the whip shall be as a caress to her spirit. And if you are diligent, the Lord will reward you with the position of Mistress of the Cellars. Do you understand? *(MARGHERITA nods.)* Sisters, you are to restrain the devil that possesses our poor sister's spirit, and no matter how much that devil cries out, you are not to let her go. For the devil will attempt to take over Sister Felice's voice, even as it has already possessed her body, and the devil can deceive the very elect. You are not to release her until I, Catherine of Siena, instructed through the Holy Spirit shall tell you.

FELICE: *(To FATHER RICORDATI.)* This little joke has gone far enough –

BENEDETTA/ST. CATHERINE: *(Cutting her off.)* Now! Apply the discipline! Sister Margherita! *(MARGHERITA whips FELICE, who is stunned.)*

FELICE: Margherita! If you strike me again—

BENEDETTA/ST. CATHERINE: Again! *(MARGHERITA hits her again. FELICE cries out involuntarily.)*

FELICE: You will never—

BENEDETTA/ST. CATHERINE: Harder! The devil speaks! Drown him out! Drown out the devil! And we will pray for the sister... *(Crossing herself, she leads the nuns, who have been swept up in the torture, in prayer.)* "In nomine Patris, et Filii, et Spiritus Sancti." *(MARGHERITA whips FELICE. FELICE, in shock, remains silent.)* "Pater noster... (Another blow.) ...qui es in caelis... (And another.)... sanctificetur nomen tuum. (Offstage, ANGELINA is heard laughing.)*

Blackout

End of Scene

ACT II

Scene 2

The interior of the sacristy of the Convent of the Mother of God, several weeks later. It's May 25, 1618, two days before the day of the Holy Trinity. A communion service for the nuns is just ending. STEFANO CECCHI is pacing in the small chamber. He pours himself some of the wine into a communion chalice and takes a drink. FATHER RICORDATI enters in full priestly regalia, carrying the host.

RICORDATI: Monsignor Cecchi! What are you doing here?

CECCHI: Waiting for you to finish your mass.

RICORDATI: *(Shocked.)* Is that the communion wine you are drinking?

CECCHI: Not a particularly good vintage—

RICORDATI: Sacrilege!

CECCHI: Sacrilege is what I have come to talk to you about... *(Draining the cup.)* What is this I hear about a wedding on the day of the Holy Trinity?

RICORDATI: The wine for the Holy Eucharist—!

CECCHI: Ricordati, what the hell is this business about a wedding the day after tomorrow? *(RICORDATI freezes.)* First you hold elections before the Abbess has even been buried, and then you go and enclose the convent suddenly, without any advance warning to any of the girls' families—so now nobody can get a word in or out, and, of course, rumors are flying, and of course, the families are all coming to me as provost—and now I hear there is going to be a wedding with Jesus... Some kind of circus with that bleeding nun—

56

RICORDATI: *(Calmly.)* Monsignor—That "bleeding nun" is our Abbess, Mother Carlini, and she has been *blessed* with the stigmata...

CECCHI: I don't care if she has been blessed with hemorrhoids— She's a *nun*—

RICORDATI: *(Quietly, folding his vestments.)* It is the will of God.

CECCHI: Says who?

RICORDATI: Saint Catherine of Siena.

CECCHI: Catherine of Siena? That wouldn't be the same Catherine of Siena who died three hundred years ago, would it?

RICORDATI: *(Patiently.)* She has been speaking to us through the body of Mother Carlini.

CECCHI: Oh, my God, Ricordati, you can't be that big a fool? *(RICORDATI draws himself up.)* Yes, you can. *(Sighing.)* All right. So what has Saint Catherine been telling you?

RICORDATI: She has told us that it is God's will that Benedetta's marriage to Christ be a public celebration, so that all may witness the Savior's joy in his Bride.

CECCHI: Oh, my God—

RICORDATI: And St. Catherine has been very specific about the arrangements for the chapel, I might add—so that nothing could be left to human error. *(CECCHI looks at him in amazement.)* Everything has been pre-ordained, as it were—down to the last detail. St. Catherine has dictated the colors of the altar cloths, the number of candles—thirty-three to be precise—

CECCHI: And have you been able to accommodate all these demands on a convent budget?

RICORDATI: *(Very pleased with himself.)* Well, Monsignor Cecchi, what we have experienced here over the last two weeks has been nothing less than a miracle, if I may say so. On not-so-grand a scale, perhaps, but just as significant—*just as significant*—as the loaves and the fishes.

CECCHI: The loaves and the fishes?

RICORDATI: As we began to borrow items from other convents, word of the wedding spread, and within days, we were inundated with beautiful tapestries to cover the chapel walls—*(Becoming excited.)* And the Prior of Pescia—just think... The Prior of Pescia!—sent us three of their own ceremonial chairs, and the Fathers of the Holy Annunciation and the convent of Santa Maria Nuova sent us candles—and, not just "candles!" You never saw anything like them... so tall and so *thick—gloria Patri et Filio* !

CECCHI: *(Cutting him off.)* The whole town knows about this?

RICORDATI: *(Holding up his hands helplessly.)* Loaves and fishes, Monsignor...

CECCHI: And, I suppose you have invited them all?

RICORDATI: *(Quoting scripture exuberantly.)* "Go ye therefore into the highways, and as many as ye shall find, bid to the marriage..."

CECCHI: And do you expect Jesus to show up?

RICORDATI: I expect that He will be present.

CECCHI: But will people actually see him?

RICORDATI: *(Smiling.)* "Blessed are the pure in heart, for they shall see God." *(RICORDATI, confident that he has prevailed, turns.)*

CECCHI: There will be no wedding. I forbid it.

RICORDATI: You have no jurisdiction over affairs of the Church.

CECCHI: Ricordati, do not make a bigger ass of yourself than you already have. The election of this Carlini girl has alienated the most wealthy and powerful family in Pescia—

RICORDATI: Our contributions from other quarters have already doubled, since "the Carlini girl" received the stigmata. Perhaps word of this latest manifestation of Divine Grace will spread beyond Pescia… perhaps even beyond Italy—! *(RICORDATI, confident that he has prevailed, turns his attention back to tidying up the sacristy. CECCHI rises to go.)*

CECCHI: Father Ricordati? *(RICORDATI turns with a smile.)* Where exactly was it that you served prior to being sent here to Pescia…? I seem to remembering hearing that you used to have your own church… Is that true? *(RICORATI, his smile fading, says nothing.)* Something about acolytes… or choirboys…?

RICORDATI: I believe that is the business of the Church, not the Provost.

CECCHI: If you choose to go through with this spectacle of a wedding against my orders, I will resort to any means within my power—if I have to interrogate every choirboy and bootblack in Pescia. *(He turns to go. Noticing the bottle of wine, he turns back.)* And, Father, I think Our Lord would appreciate a better vintage … *(He exits. Disturbed, RICORDATI watches him.)*

Blackout

End of Scene

ACT II

Scene 3

The interior of the offices of the abbess at the new Convent of the Mother of God. It very late at night, May 26, 1618, the eve of the day of the Holy Trinity. BENEDETTA is working on something at her desk. She pauses and notices her hands. She takes a small knife out and begins to reopen the wound on one hand. A soft knock is heard.

BENEDETTA: *(Surprised to be disturbed, she drops the knife.)* Just a minute! *(She grabs the knife and hides it.)* Come in... *(MEA enters with a basket that is covered with a cloth. She leaves the door ajar. BENEDETTA is annoyed.)* Sister Bartholmea... What are you doing up so late at night? The Matins bell rang hours ago... *(BENEDETTA notices that the hand she cut is bleeding onto her papers. Angry, she shoves the papers out of the way. MEA grabs the cloth from the basket and reaches over to staunch the wound.*

MEA: Wait! *(Tending the wound, MEA dabs the blood away, and then winds the cloth gently around the hand, folding BENEDETTA's fingers around the fabric for pressure. BENEDETTA is surprised by her gentleness.)* There... Now just squeeze tight, and the bleeding should stop... *(Suddenly shy about having been so forward.)* I mean, it would stop if it were ordinary bleeding... I don't know about stigmata bleeding... *(Returning BENEDETTA's hand.)*

BENEDETTA: *(Disturbed by MEA's touch.)* Why aren't you asleep?

MEA: I wanted to bake a special bread for your wedding tomorrow... But I had to wait until after Sister Maura went to bed. But I saw the candle in your window, and I thought, if you didn't mind, I would show you what I baked—

BENEDETTA: Aren't you afraid of me?

MEA: Well... *(Trying to be tactful.)* I'm more afraid of Sister Margherita... I mean, "Sister..." What's her new name?

BENEDETTA: "Sister Paolo." Why are you afraid of her?

MEA: Because sometimes she's kind, and sometimes she's mean, and I never know when she's going to be the one or the other.

BENEDETTA: But I'm just mean all the time?

MEA: *(Trapped, she struggles for a minute before responding.)* Yes... *(There is a tense silence, and then BENEDETTA begins to laugh. MEA, relieved, laughs with her.)*

BENEDETTA: What do you think of the changes since we adopted the Rules of St. Augustine?

MEA: I like them. All the convent servants, except Sister Maura, like them.

BENEDETTA: Why doesn't she like them?

MEA: Sister Maura doesn't like giving orders to Sister Felice. She says it's not natural. She says the ass doesn't give orders to the farmer.

BENEDETTA: And what do you think?

MEA: I think the ass knows more about the farmer than the farmer knows about the ass. *(BENEDETTA laughs appreciatively.)* And, now that we all wear the same habit, and the rich girls look just like us, they aren't so snotty... *(She pauses.)* But I miss the music.

BENEDETTA: May I see? *(Indicating the basket.)*

MEA: Oh...I forgot... *(She offers BENEDETTA a small loaf.)* It's rye, with garlic and salt... and I added a little saffron... for color. That's why my fingers are all stained yellow...

BENEDETTA: You have saffron in your kitchen? Can you bring me some?

MEA: You're going to bake?

BENEDETTA: I use it to... color some parchment...

MEA: I'll get it now... *(She turns, but BENEDETTA restrains her.)*

BENEDETTA: No, stay. I want you to tell me what you think of this... *(She turns back to her desk.)*

MEA: *(Alarmed.)* Of what?

BENEDETTA: A passage from the scriptures. I'm selecting the readings for the wedding.

MEA: *(Panicked.)* Oh, I can't read...

BENEDETTA: I'm going to read it to you.

MEA: I don't know anything about words... I don't think I'm the person—

BENEDETTA: You're *just* the person. I want you to stay. *(She indicates a chair. Uncomfortable MEA sits. BENEDETTA begins to read.)* "Thou hast ravished my heart, my sister, my spouse; thou hast ravished my heart... Thy lips, O my spouse, drop as the honeycomb: honey and milk are under thy tongue; and the smell of thy garments is like the smell of Lebanon./ A garden enclosed is my sister, my spouse..." *(MEA doesn't move or speak.)* What do you think?

MEA: I thought we were all sinners, that the body is filthy...

BENEDETTA: This is the scriptures, Mea. The scriptures don't lie.

MEA: I'm not educated, Mother Carlini... I'm sorry...

BENEDETTA: The word of God is not just for the educated. Our Lord chose fishermen for his disciples. He was himself a carpenter.

His word *is* for you. *(Reading again.)* "How fair is thy love, my sister..." *(MEA suddenly begins to cry. BENEDETTA watches her.)*

MEA: Forgive me, Mother. May I go? I'm sorry... Please... I need to go... *(Crying, she tries to take the basket, but BENEDETTA pulls it away.)*

BENEDETTA: Why you are crying?

MEA: I can't tell you.

BENEDETTA: You must. I am ordering you to. *(MEA shakes her head pleadingly. BENEDETTA takes her hands. MEA tries to pull away.)* What is it?

MEA: *(Blurting out.)* My love is not fair! I'm a sinner! *(She begins to sob. BENEDETTA holds her.)* I shouldn't be here. I shouldn't be a nun. You don't know. Nobody knows... I'm the worst sinner here! Don't send me away! Please, don't send me away!

BENEDETTA: Nobody's going to send you away. Just tell me what you've done.

MEA: I can't even tell Father Ricordati. I can't tell anyone. I'm so bad. I'm going to hell... *(She begins to cry again. BENEDETTA uses her bandage to wipe her eyes. This catches MEA's attention.)* Oh, your hand... I forgot all about it... *(Examining the bandage.)* How is it? Does it hurt?

BENEDETTA: *(After a moment.)* You had a baby, didn't you? *(Numb, MEA nods, keeping her head down.)* And you weren't married... *(MEA, still crying, shakes her head.)* And the father was someone you worked for... *(MEA nods.)* And he forced you. *(MEA doesn't respond to this. She continues to cry. BENEDETTA strokes MEA's head for a minute before she speaks.)* Mea, look at me. *(MEA looks up.)* It wasn't your fault.

MEA: *(After a moment of anguish.)* But I gave her away...I gave my baby away!

BENEDETTA: What were your choices?

MEA: They told me I would lose my job, if I kept her. And I couldn't let my mother find out. It would have killed her. But I lost my job anyway, and now my mother's dead, and I should never have let them take her!

BENEDETTA: You loved your daughter.

MEA: She was so tiny… She was so perfect…

BENEDETTA: Sister Bartholmea, you did nothing wrong. The father of the child was the sinner. He was the evil one. And you gave the child away in order to save the child and your mother. There is nothing to be ashamed of. Jesus understands that. He gave up his life, he suffered and died, so that we might live. You are more than worthy to be the bride of Christ.

MEA: I don't want to be anybody's bride! I want to be a virgin again! *(She begins to cry again. BENEDETTA looks at her for a long moment. Suddenly, she rises and crosses to her desk. She retrieves a paper.)*

BENEDETTA: Do you know who Saint Agnes was? *(MEA shakes her head.)* She was a saint who refused to get married, and for punishment, they sent her to a whorehouse. And do you know what she said? *(Reading.)* "I love Christ, whose bedchamber I shall enter… whom when I shall have loved I shall be chaste, when I shall have touched I shall be clean, when I shall have received him I shall be a virgin." *(BENEDETTA looks up.)* Do you understand what Saint Agnes is saying?

MEA: *(Slowly.)* That Jesus can make her a virgin again…?

BENEDETTA: That is exactly what she is saying. *(Pausing.)* Do you believe that?

MEA: Is it true?

BENEDETTA: Are you willing to receive the kind of love that St. Agnes is talking about? Are you willing to enter the bedchamber of Christ and let Him heal you with his touch?

MEA: *(Terrified.)* No!

BENEDETTA: Even if it makes you a virgin again?

MEA: I... I can't. Mother Carlini, I just can't. *(BENEDETTA waits.)* It's... it's just the thought of a man's body... *(BENEDETTA nods.)* Even if it was Jesus... I just couldn't...

BENEDETTA: What if it was a woman's body? Would a woman's body scare you?

MEA: Oh, no... Women don't scare me. They're completely different. I used to sleep with my sisters... I'm not afraid of women.

BENEDETTA: What if Jesus sent you a bridegroom in a woman's body?

MEA: How could he do that?

BENEDETTA: The scriptures say, "There is neither male nor female: for ye are all one in Christ Jesus."

MEA: I don't know...

BENEDETTA: Your body, Mea, is the Garden of Eden. This... *(She touches MEA's breasts very lightly. MEA freezes.)* ...this is paradise... and this... *(She touches her lap lightly. MEA flinches involuntarily. BENEDETTA sighs.)* You see? You see how afraid you are of your own body? I tell you it is Paradise, and you are afraid. This is the serpent, Mea. The serpent of men's sexuality that has taught us to hate our bodies... And you know after Eve had to leave the garden of Eden, there was a guard with a flaming sword to keep her from coming back. That sword, Mea, that flaming sword is ignorance and shame. That's all that is keeping women from going back to the garden that is ours, that has always been ours, because it is our bodies. Just ignorance and shame. Will you brave that sword to re-enter Paradise?

MEA: Is that what you have done?

BENEDETTA: Yes.

MEA: Then I will.

BENEDETTA: Good. Mea, let us pray. *(MEA kneels on the floor. BENEDETTA places her hand on MEA's head.)* Jesus, this is Sister Bartholmea, and she wants to become your bride also. She wants to be healed of the lusts of men, to know the perfect love that casts out fear. She wants to be restored to her virginity. And, Lord, thou who knowest all things, all secrets of the heart, thou knowest what evil has been done to her, and thou knowest that she cannot tolerate the sight or the touch of a man's body. Be thou pleased to come to her through the body of a woman, and know that I, Mother Carlini, am willing to become that vessel for your chaste desire... *(BENEDETTA opens her eyes.)* Sister Bartholmea... *(MEA opens her eyes.)* The Lord has heard your prayer.

MEA: *(Terrified.)* He has?

BENEDETTA: Jesus is going to send an angel...

MEA: An angel!

BENEDETTA: Yes, an angel. Your Lord is going to send an angel to you to be your bridegroom...

MEA: No!

BENEDETTA: Wait! Listen to me... The angel will be in my body. Now, close your eyes... *(MEA closes her eyes.)* Jesus is going to send an angel to you, Mea, a beautiful young angel. His name is Splenditello, and he has lovely golden, curly hair. He is wearing a white robe... a beautiful, soft, white robe, and the sleeves are embroidered in gold. And he has a chain, a gold chain around his neck. And in his hair there is a wreath of flowers, beautiful flowers

66

from paradise... and when he touches you, Mea, it will feel like an angel, and he will take your hands, like this... *(BENEDETTA takes MEA's hands. MEA opens her eyes.)* Close your eyes, Mea. You are to close your eyes and keep them closed, so that you will not look upon the face of your Beloved. Can you do that?

MEA: Yes, Mother Carlini. *(BENEDETTA rises and blows out the candles.)*

BENEDETTA: Keep your eyes closed. *(She takes her hands.)* Are you ready.

MEA: *(Her eyes still closed.)* Yes, Mother Carlini.

BENEDETTA: Splenditello is here. *(She raises MEA's hands to her lips and kisses them. She begins to undress MEA. ANGELINA appears at the open door. She stops to watch.)*

Blackout

End of Scene

ACT II

Scene 4

Interior of the chapel of the Convent of the Mother of God, the Day of the Holy Trinity, 1618. FELICE is on her knees washing the steps to the altar. There is medley of voices heard offstage, and then the nuns, carrying garlands of flowers, enter. MAURA is in charge of the decorating. The garlands are carried by CRISTINA, MARGHERITA, and CECILIA.

MAURA: Hurry! Hurry! We only have a few hours until the wedding. Cristina, you and Cecilia start with those pews over there, and Margherita... *(To MARGHERITA, who has spotted FELICE and is crossing to her.)* Where are you going?

MARGHERITA: Well, if it isn't Sister Michaela, down on her knees... formerly known as the great Felice di Giovanni Guerrini! Sister Michaela—who's not allowed to speak! *(FELICE ignores her. MARGHERITA turns to CECILIA.)* Cecilia... I mean, Sister Josepha... Look who's here? Don't you want to talk to your girlfriend?

MAURA: *(To MARGHERITA.)* You leave her alone! Come over here and help me with these flowers!

MARGHERITA: *(Ignoring MAURA.)* What's the matter, Cecilia? Afraid to talk to her?

MAURA: Margherita! Now!

MARGHERITA: *(To FELICE.)* It looks like your girlfriend doesn't have too much time for you, now that you're not "Felice Guerrini" anymore. Now that you're just a convent servant. *(MARGHERITA spits on the floor.)* You missed a spot. *(FELICE ignores her.)*

MAURA: Now, wasn't that nasty? And in front of the Virgin, too! You should be ashamed of yourself, Margherita Ricordati!

MARGHERITA: *(Angry, she turns to MAURA.)* I'm *Sister Paolo*, and you had better watch how you talk to me... I could report you to Mother Carlini!

MAURA: I'm not afraid of you, Margherita-Paolo-Jesus-Mary-Joseph! You were lazy and bad-tempered before we were enclosed, and now that we're an official convent, you're even worse! Now, here... You help me with this pew... *(She takes CECILIA's end of the garland and shoves it into MARGHERITA's hands.)* And, Cecilia... *(CECILIA turns to her, frightened. MAURA sends her to FELICE as an act of mercy.)* ...You just take these flowers here, and go up there by the statue and put them around the Virgin's feet. Go on... *(CECILIA crosses up to the statue, where FELICE is working. FELICE looks at her lover, but CECILIA, terrified, averts her eyes.)* Now, Cristina, have you seen Mea?

CRISTINA: She wasn't at matins this morning...

MAURA: She's not sick, is she?

CRISTINA: I don't know. She wasn't in her bed last night.

MARGHERITA: *(Turning like an inquisitor on CRISTINA.)* And how would you know if she was in her bed or not?

CRISTINA: I checked after she missed the service at matins. What is your problem?

MARGHERITA: I don't have a problem. It seems that it's girls like Cecilia... *(CECILIA turns, afraid.)* ...and Bartholmea who are the ones with the problem. *(To CECILIA.)* Cecilia, you haven't been sleeping with our little Sister Bartholmea, have you...? *(FELICE starts to get up. CECILIA steps quickly in front of her to prevent a fight.)*

CECILIA: I don't know where Sister Bartholmea is. I have not seen her since yesterday, when she was serving the evening meal. But if Sister Paolo would like for me to go and look for her...

MARGHERITA: Never mind. I'll look for her myself. I wouldn't want to be the pretense for your next assignation.

FELICE: *(Grabbing MARGHERITA.)* Apologize!

MARGHERITA: She speaks! Excuse me, Sister Michaela, but aren't you under specific orders from St. Catherine herself to shut the fuck up?

FELICE: Apologize, *puttana*!

MARGHERITA: *(To others.)* You see? She speaks—*(FELICE begins to choke her.)*

CECILIA: *(Panicked.)* Felice, don't! You could get us all in trouble! *(FELICE lets go of MARGHERITA.)*

MARGHERITA: I'm going to tell my uncle! I'm going to tell Benedetta! They'll bring in the Inquisition! They're going to tie you naked to the stake, all night and all day, and then they're going to burn you!

CECILIA: No, please, Margherita...

MARGHERITA: Oh, now, it's "No, please, Margherita!" Now, you want to be my friend. What's the matter? Can't you buy your little friendships anymore? Now that your money all goes into one pot, what are you going to use to buy me? I'm Mistress of the Cellars! I'm friends with Mother Carlini! I don't need your little bribes anymore... And your girlfriend is going to burn at the stake! But, I tell you what... Why don't you come check on my bed tonight... No harm in that, is there? *(FELICE starts to react. MARGHERITA turns to her.)* Unless you want your girlfriend to burn with you? *(FELICE freezes. MARGHERITA turns to the others.)* No harm in Sister Josepha coming to check my bed, is there? *(They are all silent.)* Good. Well, I need to make sure we've got enough wine for the feast today. A fine day for a wedding! *(She exits. CECILIA starts to cry. FELICE tries to hold her, but she moves away.)*

CRISTINA: What a bitch!

MAURA: *(Comforting CECILIA, she offers her a corner of her apron.)* Here, Cecilia. Wipe your eyes with this...

CECILIA: If Felice's family only knew...

CRISTINA: Well, they don't. None of our families know. They can't visit us, except across the grate with Margherita listening, and we're not allowed to write letters. The only person that Benedetta trusts to send into the community is Sister Bartholmea, and silly little Mea thinks Benedetta is a saint!

MAURA: And maybe she is...

CRISTINA: You can't still believe that! *(A beat.)* What? Do you think Jesus is going to come down the aisle today?

MAURA: *(Resolute in her faith.)* He might. *(CHRISTINA throws up her hands.)*

CRISTINA: Oh, my God! This... This right here is the miracle! *(She falls on her knees in front of MAURA.)*

MAURA: *(Alarmed.)* What?

CRISTINA: You... You, Maura, are the miracle. The woman who will believe anything, who will suffer anything, no matter how brutal, no matter how insane... who will never doubt, never question, never rise up, never rebel. You—St. Maura!—will always understand, always forgive, always turn the other cheek, always clean up the mess that others have made. Forever and ever. World without end. You are the bleeding statue! You are the miracle! Bless me, St. Maura, for I have sinned.

MAURA: *(Confused.)* What are you talking about?

CRISTINA: My sin, my secret... I have... I admit it! May the Lord have mercy on my soul—I have... *(She chokes.)*... common sense! *(FELICE laughs.)*

71

MAURA: *(Disgusted.)* Come on, Cecilia. We need to tend to the cooking. *(MAURA, pushing CECILIA ahead of her, exits. CRISTINA follows, laughing. After they have exited, FELICE picks up her bucket to leave. Suddenly MEA bursts in.)*

MEA: Sister Felice! Sister Felice! Have you seen Sister Maura? *(FELICE turns and just looks at her.)* I overslept and I was supposed to cook this morning! *(FELICE just looks at her.)* Oh! *(A pause.)* I forgot. You're not allowed to talk to anyone. And I'm not supposed—*(Suddenly BENEDETTA enters. She is shocked to see MEA talking with FELICE.)*

BENEDETTA: Sister Bartholmea! What are you doing?

MEA: Oh... Mother Carlini!

BENEDETTA: St. Catherine has forbidden anyone to speak to her. Have you forgotten that?

MEA: No, Mother Carlini... I just—

BENEDETTA: *(To FELICE.)* Go! You are dismissed! *(FELICE pretends to leave, but hides behind a column to witness their interaction.)* What did you tell her?

MEA: Nothing, Mother Carlini.

BENEDETTA: Are you sure?

MEA: I didn't say anything about Splenditello.

BENEDETTA: I don't know what you're talking about.

MEA: Last night—When you—I mean, when Splenditello came and—

BENDETTA: "Splenditello?"

MEA: The angel... Don't you remember? He entered your body to make love to me—

BENEDETTA: Sister Bartholmea! If the Spirit used my body to hold intercourse with you, I know nothing about it. When I am present with the Spirit, I am absent from the body. Do you understand?

MEA: *(Confused.)* I ...

BENEDETTA: You not to speak to anyone of this experience. Do you understand?

MEA: Not even Father Ricordati?

BENEDETTA: *Especially* not Father Ricordati. He is a celibate, and what you have experienced is the mystery of the Bride. He would not understand it, and he would forbid your coming to me anymore. Is that what you want?

MEA: Oh, no, Mother! I couldn't bear that! Not after last night—

BENEDETTA: Come to my rooms this evening, after the wedding. Now, Mea, I have an errand for you... *(MEA waits.)* I want you to take this note to the Sisters of Santa Maria. It's a request from St. Catherine for more candles. *(Smiling.)* She is afraid that we have underestimated our need for illumination.

MEA: Should I go now?

BENEDETTA: Have you eaten?

MEA: No...

BENEDETTA: You can eat first. Go to the refectory.

MEA: Thank you, Mother Carlini. *(She turns and exits. BENEDETTA starts to go, when suddenly ANGELINA runs in. She has a mangled garland in her hands. She stops short when she sees BENEDETTA. ANGELINA, watching BENEDETTA, crosses slowly to the statue of Mary and places the garland around Mary's neck. Her eyes on BENEDETTA, she begins to run her hands suggestively over Mary's body, while she touches herself. BENEDETTA watches her. ANGELINA makes exaggerated sounds of love-making.)*

BENEDETTA: Stop it! Angelina, stop it! *(ANGELINA becomes louder.)* Do you hear me? *(BENEDETTA grabs ANGELINA. ANGELINA looks at her and speaks slowly:)*

ANGELINA: Splenditello—! *(She pulls away and runs off.)* Splenditello! Splenditello! Splenditello!

BENEDETTA: *(In shock.)* Oh, my god. She must have seen—! *(She grabs the whip from the altar and exits, running.)* Angelina! *(FELICE steps out from behind the pillar just as CECILIA enters. Neither woman says anything for a long moment.)*

FELICE: Cecilia… *(CECILIA silences her. They stand there. FELICE reaches her arms out to her. CECILIA shakes her head. The two women just stand. CECILIA begins to cry.)* I have a plan… *(CECILIA shakes her head.)* I need your help. *(CECILIA shakes her head.)* We have to get a message to the Provost, to Monsignor Cecchi. Benedetta is sending Sister Bartholmea to another convent today to get more candles. I want you to give a note to her. Tell her that it's from "Mother Carlini." She can't read. She won't know it's not. Please… It's our only chance. If the wedding goes through, it will be too late. The whole town will believe she's a saint. *(CECILIA looks at her.)* I know. I know it's dangerous for you. But you're already in danger. *(CECILIA covers her face with shame.)* Please…

CECILIA: *(Turning away, in a quiet voice.)* I'm not brave like you are.

FELICE: Come with me… I'll write the note. I'm not brave, Cecilia… just proud. *(They exit.)*

Blackout

End of Scene

ACT II

Scene 5

The interior of the sacristy, a few hours before the scheduled wedding. The figure of BENEDETTA is seen kneeling with her back to the audience. FATHER RICORDATI enters. He is surprised to see her there.

FATHER RICORDATI: Benedetta? *(She turns to face him. Her forehead is streaming blood, as are her hands.)* Good Lord... *(She bows her head. He collects himself.)*

BENEDETTA: Forgive me, Father... I didn't want to disturb you, but—

FATHER RICORDATI: *(Suddenly skeptical.)* The crown of thorns...? *(He shakes his head.)*

BENEDETTA: Father, someone is trying to sabotage the plans for Our Lord's wedding today... They left this note on my door... You can see that they have forged your name—

FATHER RICORDATI: *(Cutting her off.)* It isn't forged.

BENEDETTA: But—

FATHER RICORDATI: The wedding has been cancelled. The Provost has asked me to cancel it.

BENEDETTA: I don't understand... It's scheduled to take place in less than an hour... All of Pescia has been invited—

FATHER RICORDATI: *(Firmly.)* The wedding is cancelled.

BENEDETTA: But, look... *(She holds out her left hand. He looks.)* See how the skin glows bright yellow, as if a ring of gold were around it? I tried to wash it off, but the more I rubbed, the brighter it shone... Is this not my wedding band, Father, from my Holy Bridegroom?

FATHER RICORDATI: *(Faltering.)* It would appear to be some form of manifestation...

BENEDETTA: What will happen to us if we disobey Saint Catherine? What will happen when my Bridegroom comes and finds that we are not prepared? *(RICORDATI does not know what to say.)* Perhaps, if we could show the Provost my ring...?

FATHER RICORDATI: No! *(A pause.)* This has been my decision. *(Preaching.)* "The children of this world marry and are given in marriage. But they that are accounted worthy to obtain that world and the resurrection from the dead, neither marry nor are given in marriage..."

BENEDETTA: *(Cutting him off.)* But Saint Catherine—

FATHER RICORDATI: *(Cutting her off.)* Saint Catherine is of the spirit world.

BENEDETTA: *(Head bowed in humility.)* Your Grace, I *have* been elected abbess...

FATHER RICORDATI: I am sorry, but I have made up my mind. The wedding is cancelled. I'll have Margherita meet the guests at the gate and tell them to go home, that there's been a mistake... It's very simple. *(Suddenly BENEDETTA falls to the floor in a faint. RICORDATI watches her suspiciously. She rises suddenly in the full vigor of an outraged ST. CATHERINE.)*

BENEDETTA/ST. CATHERINE: Kneel! *(The priest involuntarily takes a step back.)* It is I, Saint Catherine of Siena, who commands you to *kneel*! *(He stands his ground. With a wrenching cry, BENEDETTA sinks to the floor, clutching her heart.)*

BENEDETTA: Oh... Oh... Help me! It is the Sacred Heart of Jesus in me... *(FATHER RICORDATI stands in silence. BENEDETTA extends her hand to him. He does not take it. In a loud voice, she begins to cry out for MEA.)* Sister Bartholmea! Sister Bartholmea!

Help! Help me! *(After a few seconds, MEA rushes in. She is shocked to see her beloved abbess on the floor.)*

MEA: Mother Carlini! What is it?

BENEDETTA: The Sacred Heart of Jesus...

MEA: *(Turning to RICORDATI.)* Father, what should we do?

BENEDETTA: Hold me, Sister Bartholmea... hold me... I am dying... *(MEA rushes to hold her.)*

FATHER RICORDATI: *(Coldly.)* Mother Carlini is not dying. I'm sure she will be fine again in a few minutes. *(He turns to go. Just then, BENEDETTA utters a cry and slumps, apparently dead.)*

MEA: She's dead! Oh, my God! Mother Carlini! Mother! Oh, Father... She's dead!

FATHER RICORDATI: *(Furious, to BENEDETTA.)* Open your eyes!

MEA: *(Frantic.)* She's dead...

FATHER RICORDATI: Benedetta Carlini, open your eyes!

MEA: *(Whimpering.)* She's dead...

FATHER RICORDATI: I command you to *open your eyes!* *(BENEDETTA's eyes fly open.)*

MEA: She's alive...

BENEDETTA: *(Getting her bearings.)* You raised me from the dead, Father! You brought me back to life!

FATHER RICORDATI: Don't be ridiculous! You just fainted, that's all. Get up!

BENEDETTA: *(To MEA.)* You saw it, didn't you? You were a witness! I was dead and it was Father Ricordati's command that brought me back to life…

MEA: Yes, Mother! I saw it!

FATHER RICORDATI: *(To BENEDETTA.)* Heresy! *(Lecturing.)* Only Jesus can raise the dead.

BENEDETTA: *(To MEA.)* Mea… Do you understand what Father Ricordati is saying?

MEA: What?

BENEDETTA: That you are not to tell anyone what you have just witnessed here—If the Church were to find out, they could burn Father Ricordati at the stake for heresy—

FATHER RICORDATI: *(Screaming in frustration.)* You weren't dead!

BENEDETTA: *(Cutting him off.)* Forgive me, Father, but if I was not dead, how was it that I was in Purgatory? How was it that I saw my father's soul come to me and beg forgiveness for his sins?

FATHER RICORDATI: *(Coldly.)* Perhaps you have an over-active imagination.

BENEDETTA: *(Raising a bloody palm.)* And this? Is this my imagination? Or this? *(She indicates the ring, which MEA sees for the first time.)*

MEA: A ring! There's a ring of gold on your finger! *(FATHER RICORDATI turns to leave.)*

BENEDETTA: Father! Is the wedding still to be cancelled?

FATHER RICORDATI: *(Without turning.)* Yes.

BENEDETTA: *(Lowering her eyes.)* Then I cannot protect you.

FATHER RICODATI: *(Wheeling around in shock.)* What? Are you threatening me?

BENEDETTA: *(Humbly.)* I am only trying to protect you, as you have tried to protect me. *(He looks at her and then at MEA. BENEDETTA , after a moment, turns to MEA.)* Did the Sisters of Santa Maria give you the candles that I requested?

MEA: Yes, Mother.

BENEDETTA: Good. Take them to Sister Maura and tell her that we will use them for the wedding feast. *(MEA looks at FATHER RICORDATI. He is speechless.)* Go on, Sister Bartholmea.

MEA: Yes, Mother. *(MEA exits.)*

BENEDETTA: Father, Saint Catherine has asked that the scriptural selections for the ceremony be taken from the Song of Solomon. I trust that your earlier objection to those passages has been withdrawn. *(He stares at her. She bows to him and exits.)*

FATHER RICORDATI: I've been a fool... *(He quickly pours himself a glass of wine.)* ... A fool! *(He drinks the wine, and then quickly begins to unwind the rope tie that is around his waist.)*

Blackout

End of Scene

ACT II

Scene 6

The interior of the chapel, the Day of the Holy Trinity. The set is rotated so that the audience constitutes the congregation of townspeople. MAURA, MEA, CRISTINA, FELICE, and CECILIA are gathered with the other nuns in the aisle, lining up for the procession. FELICE, still being shunned, stands apart from the others. MARGHERITA enters.

MARGHERITA: Has anybody seen Father Ricordati? *(Silence.)* He was supposed to meet us here for the procession. *(Silence.)* Mother Carlini is not going to be happy about this. And what about the Provost? Has anybody seen him? *(Silence. FELICE looks at CECILIA. CECILIA tries to indicate that she did deliver the note. MEA raises her hand.)* What?

MEA: *(Frightened.)* I delivered Mother's note to the Provost this afternoon. I delivered it right into his hands. I took it to him right after Sister Cecilia gave it to me. Will you tell her that? *(CECILIA is terrified.)*

MARGHERITA: *(Annoyed.)* She didn't say anything about any note to me...

CRISTINA: What if Father Ricordati doesn't show up?

MARGHERITA: The wedding will go on as planned.

MAURA: But we can't have a service without a priest! Who ever heard of such a thing?

CRISTINA: Who ever heard of a wedding without a bridegroom?

MARGHERITA: Quiet! Here she comes! *(BENEDETTA enters, dressed all in white. Her hands are bandaged, but the blood has begun to seep through. There is blood on her forehead, as before. Her head is bowed as if in prayer or in a trance, and the nuns are awed by her demeanor.)* Mother Carlini... *(She looks up.)* No one has seen Father Ricordati, and the Provost is not here. Should we wait for them?

BENEDETTA: Saint Catherine is insistent that nothing should delay the wedding.

MARGHERITA: *(To the nuns.)* Get in your lines. Get in your lines! *(The nuns line up. BENEDETTA nods to MARGHERITA, who signals them to begin. Marching down the aisle in pairs, they sing in plainchant. FELICE, alone, follows. The sisters take their places at the side of the altar. After the nuns are in place, BENEDETTA makes her way down the aisle by herself. The music stops as she reaches the front of the church. She kneels before the statue of Mary. MARGHERITA steps forward.)*

MARGHERITA: Father Ricordati regrets that he will not be present today. It is the will of Our Lord Jesus that the ceremony proceed without him. *(Suddenly BENEDETTA rises and turns, her hands unwrapped and streaming blood. She raises them above her head. Crossing to the lectern, her hands still uplifted, she begins to read:)*

BENEDETTA: "I am come into my garden, my sister, my spouse: I have gathered my myrrh with my spice... O beloved." *(With a cry, she faints. Suddenly, she rises, her back to the the congregation. She begins to address them with a male voice.)*

BENEDETTA/ JESUS: *(Crossing himself.)* "I am come that ye might have Life, and that ye might have it more abundantly." *(MAURA gasps and falls to her knees.)* "This is my Beloved..." *Suddenly CECCHI appears at the back of the chapel, followed by two of his men.)*

CECCHI: Stop! *(BENEDETTA turns in surprise and faces him.)* Where is your priest? Where is Ricordati? *(BENEDETTA faints. CECCHI turns to MARGHERITA.)* Margherita! *(MARGHERITA, terrified, steps forward.)* Go find your uncle! *(She runs off. CECCHI strides to the front of the church, where he turns to address the people.)* What the hell is going on here? *(CECILIA and FELICE exchange glances.)* Have you women all gone mad?

MEA: *(Stepping forward grabs his sleeve.)* Excuse me, Sir— Mother Carlini has fainted...

CECCHI: *(Shaking her off, he produces the note.)* Leave her! I have come here with officials from the Inquisition, and I ask you all to answer to these charges... that your "abbess" Benedetta Carlini is guilty of claiming stigmata when she wounds her own hands, of fasting when she has been seen stealing food at night, of reinstating the discipline when she herself never applies it to herself, of removing the golden candelabra from the altar to use in her own room, of appropriating the convent infirmary as a suite of private rooms, and of practicing witchcraft in the form of demonic possession and diabolic visions... and insisting that these are a special grace! And now, today, she has had the effrontery to stage a mock wedding between herself—trafficker with the devil—and the Son of God! *(CECCHI turns to BENEDETTA.)* Benedetta Carlini, what do you say to these charges? *(She rises slowly, clinging to the lectern for support.)*

BENEDETTA: What can I, the lowliest handmaiden of the Lord, say when My Lord and Savior, my great exemplar, was silent before his accusers? *(She bows her head.)*

CECCHI: *(Unimpressed.)* So they're true?

BENEDETTA: If they are, then I have been cruelly deceived in my faith. The stigmata arrived on the very day of Mother Piera's death, when the whole congregation was in deep mourning and prayer for some sign of guidance. If I was seen taking food at night, it was only to minister to one of the sisters who was sick. The wounds of the stigmata are as real as the scars on my back, which modesty prevents me from displaying. There were rumors of a break-in at the chapel, and so I thought it best to remove the gold candelabra to my chambers, to guard them. And, as the sick prefer their own beds, I temporarily moved into the infirmary so that I would not disturb the sleep of my sisters with my prayers and the visions, which frequently keep me up throughout the night. If these visions are of the devil and not from God, Monsignor, I know not how to answer, except that I have been deceived in my very soul, because the visions have always resulted in a greater desire to be good and a deeper, holier love for my Lord Jesus. *(CECCHI is taken aback for a moment. The nuns are mumuring. Suddenly, MARGHERITA rushes in.)*

MARGHERITA: Monsignor!

CECCHI: What is it?

MARGHERITA: The doors to the sacristy have been locked from the inside—

CECCHI: *(Turning to his men.)* Quickly! Men—break down those doors! *(The two men exit with MARGHERITA. CECCHI turns to BENEDETTA.)* What do you know of this?

BENEDETTA: Nothing, Your Grace. Father Ricordati was to have conducted the service today. *(Just then, a terrible scream is heard offstage. ANGELINA runs in. She is half-naked and covered with blood. She has been brutally whipped. Her hands are still tied together, but she has chewed through the ropes that confined her. Seeing all the people in the chapel, she freezes. Shocked, no one moves. Slowly, ANGELINA raises her bound arms and points at BENEDETTA.)*

ANGELINA: Splenditello!

CECCHI: Who is this?

BENEDETTA: Sister Angelina, Monsignor. She is crazy. We have to bind her to keep her from hurting herself. *(Turning to the shocked nuns.)* Sister Maura and Sister Cristina, tend to Angelina! *(MAURA and CRISTINA cross to ANGELINA, who is frozen in an attitude of accusation. She resists them violently.)*

ANGELINA: Splenditello! Splenditello! Splenditello! *(The two women manage to drag her off, as she is still pointing and repeating the name of her abuser.)*

CECCHI: Who is this Splenditello?

BENEDETTA: Part of her madness...

MEA: *(Rising suddenly.)* I know who he is!

BENEDETTA: Sister Bartholmea, it is a heresy for a nun to speak in the chapel—

MEA: I *will* speak, even if they burn me at the stake—Splenditello is an angel...

BENEDETTA: Mea is very ignorant and superstitious—*(Suddenly MARGHERITA runs in.)*

MARGHERITA: Monsignor! Monsignor! *(CECCHI turns.)* He's dead! My uncle is dead! He has hanged himself in the sacristy! *(The two men enter carrying the body of FATHER RICORDATI.)*

CECCHI: *(To MEA.)* Who is Splenditello?

MEA: I know who Splenditello is, because he is my lover! I know who he is, because he has kissed me, he has told me I was beautiful, he has made love to me. He said he was an angel sent by God, he said he was my bridegroom, and that it was the will of Jesus that I give my body to him. I know who he is, because, in my foolishness, I believed him, and I am damned forever because I loved him.

CECCHI: But who is he?

MEA: He is a devil disguised as an angel. He is an enemy disguised as a friend. He is a man disguised in the body of a woman. *(She turns to BENEDETTA.)* She is Splenditello!

CECCHI: Benedetta Carlini, you are under arrest. I order you confined to your cell until the Church shall convene a session of the Inquisition to try you for your heresy and your lechery. Take her away! *(His men set the body down and begin to cross to BENEDETTA. She turns to the crowd in desperation.)*

BENEDETTA: Don't touch me! *(Backing away.)* Provost, the day shall come when you will pray on your knees for my forgiveness—you and all Pescia, for the Lord, in his anger, will smite you and all your kin! If you lay a hand on me, I swear to you by God and all his angels that I shall live to see every third one of you die by the plague! *(She is dragged off.)*

Blackout

End of Act II

ACT III

Scene 1

It is Ascension Day, 1631. Thirteen years have passed since the arrest of BENEDETTA. The scene takes place in the courtyard of the Convent of the Mother of God. MAURA stands at a long table, in front of an array of herbs and bowls. MAURA has aged visibly. She is in the process of pounding a pile of broken glass with a pestle. CRISTINA enters.

CRISTINA: Maura, have you seen Margherita?

MAURA: *(Absorbed in her work.)* No...

CRISTINA: She's our porter, but she's never at the gate when she's supposed to be. Bishop Cecchi has come... *(Noticing the broken glass.)* What are you doing?

MAURA: Shhh! It's a secret.

CRISTINA: Why are you grinding up broken glass?

MAURA: I'm making an unguent.

CRISTINA: You're making an unguent out of ground glass?

MAURA: Of course not! I'm grinding up the glass to *put in* the unguent. *(CRISTINA looks at her.)* Well, you can't just rub broken glass on your skin! It won't stay there... You have to mix it up with other things.

CRISTINA: What other things?

MAURA: *(Pointing to a pile of herbs and a bowl of mud-like contents.)* Poison ivy and cow manure.

CRISTINA: This is a joke? *(MAURA smiles.)* You know that Mother Felice banned the whips and the hair shirts and fasting thirteen years ago. We haven't had any "humiliations of the flesh" since they arrested Benedetta and locked her in her cell—

MAURA: *(Whispering.)* But this is to treat the plague.

CRISTINA: The plague!

MAURA: It's a recipe that's been in the family for a hundred and fifty years.

CRISTINA: But there's no plague here...

MAURA: Yet! But it's already in Milan and Modena—and yesterday the wine merchant told me there were rumors it had reached Florence.

CRISTINA: Florence!

MAURA: *(Nodding.)* Florence. But we don't need to worry, because I have the cure.

CRISTINA: *(Pacing.)* So the plague has already reached Florence... That must be why Bishop Cecchi has come...

MAURA: *(Pounding.)* Mother Carlini warned us.

CRISTINA: *(Noticing a decanter.)* And what's this?

MAURA: Turpentine.

CRISTINA: That's crazy! Your cure is worse than the disease! *(MAURA keeps pounding.)* But that's the point, isn't it? You're going to make dying of the plague feel like a mercy... Oh, my God! Has everybody gone crazy? It's *rats*! It's a disease spread by *rats*! *(Suddenly CECILIA enters.)*

CECILIA: Does anyone know where Margherita is? Bishop Cecchi was at the gate, and I let him in, but now there is a crowd that's beginning to gather... They're calling for Benedetta!

CRISTINA: *(Shaking her head, in reference to calling for BENEDETTA.)* Ground glass…

CECILIA: Do you think Bishop Cecchi will release her?

CRISTINA: Why not? What difference could it make now? She's too weak from her imprisonment to cause any trouble.

CECILIA: Listen! They're breaking down the gate! *(Sounds of a mob.)*

CRISTINA: Quick! Gather everyone into the chapel! We can barricade the doors with the pews… *(MAURA tries to gather up her mortar.)* Leave it! *(She pushes the old woman ahead of her, as they all exit. After a moment MARGHERITA stumbles on. She has aged appallingly and is very drunk.)*

MARGHERITA: *(Talking to herself.)* "Where is Margherita?" "Where is our porter?" *(Yelling.)* Do you think I can hold the gates against the whole town? I can't protect you anymore! *(Seeing the bottle of turpentine.)* What's this? Someone's gotten careless… But I won't tell, because there won't be anything to tell… There won't be anything *left* to tell… *(She tips it back and swallows a draft. Clutching her throat, she falls over in agony. As she is dying, ANGELINA enters with a handful of wildflowers. She drops them on MARGHERITA. The sound of the mob swells.)*

Blackout

End of Scene

ACT III

Scene 2

The office of the Abbess of the Convent of God, the same day. CECCHI, now a bishop, is meeting with FELICE, who is now the abbess of the convent. The muted sound of the mob is heard in the background.

FELICE: She won't do it.

CECCHI: She has to. I'm telling you, the people are going to riot. The whole town is gathering outside those gates. They're threatening to burn down the convent.

FELICE: Benedetta hasn't spoken a word to anyone in thirteen years, and she's dying now—

CECCHI: Dying?—Not—

FELICE: No, it's not plague. She's coughing up blood and hasn't been eating for weeks. She can't live much longer.

CECCHI: Still, there must be something she wants…

FELICE: Revenge. That's what Benedetta wants. That's what she's always wanted.

CECCHI: Well, she's going to get her wish, unless we can figure out a way to arrange a public reconciliation with her… That's what the people want to see. They're not going home until they get it.

FELICE: *(Shaking her head.)* After everything, they still believe in her.

CECCHI: Ricordati was right. They want miracles. *(Pacing.)* Do you know the Grand Duke of Tuscany tried to organize a board of public health at the first reports of plague…? He sent officers out to patrol the streets… sending the stricken to the plague hospitals, burning their belongings, disinfecting and boarding up their homes.

He quarantined the families, and then he banned public sermons and processions.

FELICE: Did it work?

CECCHI: Did it work? *(A bitter laugh.)* The Pope disbanded his board of health and ordered the Duke to do public penance. And now the Church is holding religious processions daily, so, of course, the disease has spread to every corner of the city. *(He sighs. There is a roar from outside.)* I fear the plague has already reached us, and that plague is ignorance.

Blackout

End of Scene

ACT III

Scene 3

The lights come up on the interior of a prison cell in a convent in Pescia, Italy. It is Ascension Day, 1631. The cell has only a bed, a table and a chair. There is a figure in the bed. This is BENEDETTA CARLINI. She is 36, but appears older, because she is ill with consumption and close to dying. Outside the cell is the sound of a mob rioting. They are calling for "Santa Benedetta." BENEDETTA, with great effort, rises and crosses to her window. She is looking out the window, when suddenly the door opens. FELICE enters. BENEDETTA turns.

FELICE: Sister Benedetta... *(A long pause.)* Sister—*(BENEDETTA holds up a hand.)*

BENEDETTA: I hear you. *(Another long pause.)*

FELICE: I've come—

BENEDETTA: *(Cutting her off.)* I know why you've come. You don't like waiting, do you? But I've had to wait thirteen years...

FELICE: Sister Benedetta—

BENEDETTA: *Saint* Benedetta.

FELICE: *(After a pause.)* How are you?

BENEDETTA: *(Another long pause.)* Dying. But then you knew that...

FELICE: We are all sorry that you are so ill.

BENEDETTA: Yes, I am sure that you are, because it appears that, when the townspeople of Pescia hear that I am dead, they will burn down the convent. *(A moment of silence as the sound of the mob swells.)*

FELICE: What do you want?

BENEDETTA: What do *I* want? *(Smiling with pleasure.)* I *have* what I want... *(She pauses to listen.)* I could not ask for a more perfect revenge. You coming here to beg for my forgiveness, so that the good people of Pescia can go home in peace, believing that the Angel of Death will pass over their homes... Pray with me, Sister Felice. Get on your knees and let us pray together to know the will of God. *(Warily, FELICE kneels with BENEDETTA.)* Pray!

FELICE: *"Ave Maria, gratia plena, Dominus tecum"* —

BENEDETTA: *(Rising.)* A vision! I have a vision! Oh... I can barely make it out... Shadows and shapes... Oh, Sister Felice! You will burn to death! You and all the sisters will burn to death! *(Coming out of her trance, she begins to laugh.)* Can you imagine the horror of being burned alive...? Of course you can, because you have made a life study of hellfire, haven't you? You've been teaching it to innocent children and browbeaten converts for centuries, haven't you? And now you're going to know what it feels like first-hand. Listen...! *(She pauses.)* When I die, they will breach the gates, and then you will face a mob of people who are enraged and terrified, because they are starting to get sick. And they will be convinced that the convent is evil and that you are all possessed by the devil. They will know that when they rip off your clothing, and when they violate you in every conceivable way, when they beat you with clubs and stab you with knives... they will know that they are doing the will of God! You will barricade yourselves in the chapel with the statue of the Holy Mother. You will gather around her wooden image like superstitious children, won't you? And you will hear them nailing the windows shut, as they pile up logs around the doors and throw flaming sticks on the roof. And you will pray, Sister Felice. You will pray and you will encourage your little flock of frightened sheep to pray with you. You will pray for your wretched souls, because it will be too late for your bodies... Already you will be feeling the heat. It will feel like an oven, an oven for baking sinners. You will choke on the smoke that is seeping in under the door and around the eaves, filling the chancel like an antichamber of hell... Someone's hair will burst into flame... and then her clothing... and you will tear your clothes off... and your skin will blister and blacken—And in your last agonies of tortured flesh, you will turn to the Holy Mother of God, and she will be going up in flames to meet you...to meet you in hell! *(She laughs and begins to cough.)*

FELICE: So there is nothing we can do?

BENEDETTA: *(There is a long silence. FELICE turns to go. As she reaches the door, BENEDETTA speaks.)* Send Bartholmea to me. *(Pause.)* Oh, no... wait! The Inquisition has threatened to burn her alive if she tries to see me. *(BENEDETTA laughs. Her laughter turns into a paroxysm of coughing.)*

FELICE: I'll send her. *(She exits. BENEDETTA turns to the window, where the cries of "Santa Benedetta" continue. Slowly the door to her cell opens and MEA steps into the dim light. BENEDETTA stares at her in silence for a long moment.)* Sister Bartholmea... and after only thirteen years. *(After a pause.)*

MEA: Mother Guerrini—.

BENEDETTA: She sent you to ask for my pardon. *(Pausing.)* *(MEA, terrified, does not respond.)* Don't be scared, little Mea. *(Sighing.)* You forgot me, didn't you?

MEA: *(After a long pause.)* No.

BENEDETTA: You are lying, but I forgive you...

MEA: I'm not lying!

BENEDETTA: No? *(Pausing.)* What do you remember?

MEA: Our sin.

BENEDETTA: "Our sin." Funny... What I remember is your pleasure.

MEA: It was a sin.

BENEDETTA: *(A beat.)* The scriptures say that all of our sins can be forgiven except one. Do you know which one that is?

MEA: The sin against the Holy Spirit.

BENEDETTA: Do you know what that is? *(MEA looks down.)* It is to deny who you are. I am the only woman in this convent who has never denied herself.

MEA: You told me you were Splenditello!

BENEDETTA: *(Thundering.)* I *am* Splenditello! I am *more* Splenditello than I am Benedetta! You should know that... *(Coughing from the exertion.)*

MEA: *(After a long pause.)* Will you grant us the pardon?

BENEDETTA: *(A test.)* Will you kiss me? *(MEA freezes. BENEDETTA laughs.)* There's your answer. *(BENEDETTA crosses to the door and flings it open. FELICE, CECCHI, MAURA, CRISTINA, CECILIA, and the others are gathered at the door.)* Oh, so you're all here... Good! You can all hear what I have to say after my thirteen years of living death—(*Suddenly the ghost of the ABBESS appears. She approaches BENEDETTA.)* No! No! What are *you* doing here? *(She shrinks away from the ABBESS.)*

CECILIA: *(To FELICE.)* Who is she talking to?

ABBESS: Benedetta, child...

BENEDETTA: No! I was never a child! *(The ABBESS continues to approach her.)* I told you that... I was never... *(She puts her hands up to block the approach of the ABBESS.)*... a child! *(The ABBESS presses her palms to BENEDETTA's. BENEDETTA lets out a cry of a lifetime of anguish.)*

MAURA: She sees something! *(The ABBESS releases BENEDETTA who falls back on the bed. The ABBESS disappears.)*

94

CECILIA: No! She can't die yet...! *(BENEDETTA's hands fall open. She has bleeding wounds on both palms.)*

MAURA: Look!

MEA: Where?

MAURA: She still has the stigmata!

CECILIA: You mean she's still *faking* the stigmata!

FELICE: *(Slowly approaching the body.)* No... She's not faking... I saw her hands just minutes ago. *(Lifting her hands.)* There's nothing in the cell she could have used for cutting... *(MAURA crosses herself.)*

CRISTINA: *(Checking for a neck pulse, she turns to the ABBESS.)* I don't know about the stigmata, but her death is real. *(Suddenly the sound of the crowd swells. They are calling for "Santa Benedetta.")*

CECILIA: *(Panicked.)* What are we going to do? They're calling for Saint Benedetta, and she's dead!

FELICE: Maura—quickly! You and Cecilia and Mea carry the body... Hurry! We will form a procession. Sister Benedetta has forgiven us, and the stigmata is the sign that God has heard her prayer. The people will believe us when they see her hands. *(Quickly, FELICE, CECILIA, MEA and MAURA pick up the body.)*

CECILIA: *(To FELICE.)* We are saved! Oh, thank God... We are saved! *(They exit with the body, leaving CRISTINA on the stage.)*

CRISTINA: *(Watching their exit.)* Saved... Saved from our superstitious fears by the stories we tell ourselves. *(Turning slowly to the audience.)* But the plague is already in Florence... *(She turns and exits. The sound of ANGELINA's laughter is heard.)*

Blackout

End of Play

www.ingramcontent.com/pod-product-compliance
Lightning Source LLC
Chambersburg PA
CBHW030348290526
45785CB00004B/1650